Good morning, brother pilgrim,
pray tell me where you're bound.
Tell me where you're travelling to
on the disenchanted ground.

My name it is poor pilgrim,
to Canaan I am bound,
travelling through this wilderness
on the disenchanted ground.

— Trad.

Enchanted Ground

Enchanted Ground

Growing Roots in a Broken World

Steven Lovatt

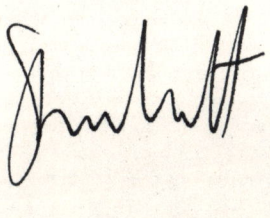

PARTICULAR BOOKS

an imprint of

PENGUIN BOOKS

PARTICULAR BOOKS

UK | USA | Canada | Ireland | Australia
India | New Zealand | South Africa

Particular Books is part of the Penguin Random House group of companies
whose addresses can be found at global.penguinrandomhouse.com.

Penguin Random House UK
One Embassy Gardens, 8 Viaduct Gardens, London SW11 7BW

penguin.co.uk

First published in Great Britain by Particular Books 2025

001

Set in 12.5/14.75pt Fournier MT Pro
Typeset by Jouve (UK), Milton Keynes
Printed and bound in Great Britain by Clays Ltd, Elcograf S.p.A.

The authorized representative in the EEA is Penguin Random House Ireland,
Morrison Chambers, 32 Nassau Street, Dublin D02 YH68

A CIP catalogue record for this book is available from the British Library

ISBN: 978–0–241–56138–6

To my family – past, present and future

Credo: Buzzard and Moon

I have left the others sleeping and gone out early by myself. The wet, weary buildings, heavy with rain and dreaming, are forgotten behind. There are no people awake but me. The hill grass is rough and the sky pale blue with a white flake of moon still caught there. I am in a landscape of mountains and rocky high pasture. Not that I think of it as a landscape: it is simply where I am, which for once is also where I am meant to be. Dilapidated stone walls mark what used to be fields, but now sheep flow at will through the gaps. The air is crisp and clean, like the white flesh of a perfect apple, and every cell of my body is singing the same song as the black streamlets that corkscrew down from the higher hills. I feel too alive to walk, and soon I am springing pell-mell over tussocks and loose, ankle-turning stones. Nocturnal coolness still steeps in the hollow places, but it is summer and the air is warming as it rises. The only sounds are a distant skylark, the dark beat of blood in my ears, and my rough breathing, regular except when I leap to avoid a spill of scree or an iron-hard rowan root.

Then, over the ridge ahead, a thrilling silhouette: a buzzard! It shapes closer until I can see the brown on its broad wings and a band of brindled silver across its chest. What happens next is hard to explain. It seems that the whole of the land and sky is centred in that shape, which is also like the pupil of a gigantic eye through which my own vision is magnified a thousandfold.

I feel something growing inside me, a feeling that I have never experienced since with half the intensity. But it would be more true to say that I *am* the feeling: a pure, irrepressible feeling of belonging. I have stopped dead still on the sheep-track to watch the bird, but I feel with a certain sudden knowledge that I and she are the same. All of my attention is centred on her as she soars. I'm a slow grower. My voice has not yet broken, and back home I try to impress my parents and sister with an imitation of a buzzard's cry. Now the force inside me takes the shape of the cry, and at the top of my voice I let out: *pee-yoo! pee-yoo!*

And she hears me. Her body turns, and she answers *pee-yoo!* I cry again, and again she replies. I am vibrating like a javelin when it hits the earth. She is not far away now, just arcing over the nearest green hill, beating darkly about the thumbnail moon, and I run again, not caring now about stone or root, and as I run I call all the time, and she answers *pee-yoo! pee-yoo!* I run and run towards her, but when I reach the top of the hill I see that it isn't the top at all, and that the buzzard is in fact over the next ridge beyond. Now she is looping away, still crying, and at last she disappears over a bald summit, leaving me on the hill, legs dripping with black sedge-water, weeping like a madman, supercharged with love.

Since then, I have known, though I have often mislaid the knowledge, that my true identity is outside myself and is shared in other things. That is why, in all the paid jobs I have ever had to do, though I have not shirked, I have been withheld always in irony. Probably for my whole life since I was first taken into the Staffordshire woods as an infant, strapped to my mother's chest, but certainly since the experience on a Welsh hillside I have just described, my allegiance has lain elsewhere. I cannot serve two masters, and my loyalty is for the venerable institution of Buzzard and Moon.

Part I

'A man is so lost in his own life.'

— *Aleksander Wat*

I

In March 2019, I caught a train from south Wales to Staffordshire
to visit my maternal grandmother, who a week before had been
taken into a nursing home. She was born in 1921 and now her long
life was nearly over. Being a weekday, the carriage was quiet, and
the few passengers were bent over their phones, lifting their heads
only when the trolley was pushed by. I could have thought about
Grandma, but my mind felt scoured blank. With each lurch of the
train my temple was knocked against the cold, dirty glass that I
stared through at the pylons and the waste ground heaped with
shipping containers, the thickset empty chapels, the wet fields of
yellow green. When sunlight thinned the clouds it made a weak
shadow of the train speeding past newbuilds, and drew desultory
flashes from rainwater lying in puddles beside the tracks. When
it shone brighter I closed my eyes and a script of tree shadows
rippled behind my eyelids. Whenever we approached a station
the same effect was created by gantries, spike-topped fencing and
video cameras on long metal poles. I remember thinking that it is
a sad country in which such ugliness can be made and the people
accept it. The train shook north and I watched as the white
flowers on the blackthorn hedges crept back into their twigs. By
the time I reached the Midlands the seasons had reversed. The
hedges were wet and dark and bare. It was winter.

At the final station my mother waited on the platform in a
blue anorak. Her hair was white and disorderly with wind, but

the inside of her car was very tidy. Between October and spring there is generally a satsuma in the cupholder by the gear stick, and now there were two. I looked at them and grinned and then we set off. I have never learned to drive.

The nursing home is a grand old building with medieval-looking chimney stacks and a wide lawn embayed in gravel. It would better suit a coach and four than a Škoda. Inside, there's a spiral staircase and, unremarkably as in a dream, Grandma is on the first floor. The nurses are kind. Grandma is alright, but they're having trouble persuading her to eat, bless her. Grandma is lying on her back with her eyes closed, but she opens them when Mum speaks. I josh her a little, to get her to eat and because I am desolate at seeing her there. The care worker brings soup and Grandma pretends to drink some while we pretend not to notice. She doesn't want to be here. She has lived all her life five miles away, in Eardlem, in her own house. She has given up, and is indifferent. Her face is resigned. I love her so much. We stay for twenty minutes and then Grandma opens her eyes again, smiles weakly and says, 'Right, you can bugger off now.'

By early summer Grandma had become weaker and confused. I travelled up again and saw her a few days before she died. She called me John, my grandad's name. He had passed away thirty years earlier. On my final visit to their house in Eardlem, Grandma told me that they had met in a department store just after the war while she was a shop assistant and he was delivering carpets. With their friends he took her to tea dances at the big house in Trentham, and they picnicked and laughed and flirted in the sun in those beautiful gardens with their fountains and clipped hedges of yew and trellises of roses that perfume the air in late summer. Then she'd taken a photograph out of an envelope in a drawer, to show me. The men all wore suit jackets and the women were in dresses. 'They were good times,' she'd told me. 'We were quite carefree.' Now Grandma was small and silent, sitting in an armchair wearing a blue cardigan. I knew I wouldn't see her again, so before we left I held her shoulder for a few seconds through the cardigan. I'd never held her for so long all my adult life, nor seen anyone else do so.

Then it was her funeral. This time my wife drove us up with the kids. They played tag in the crematorium carpark, not knowing if they should, or what to do otherwise; but the little one, Thomas, threw handfuls of carpark gravel up with all his force, and laughed to see it come down again in hissing showers. And my eyes that had travelled up with the flying stones saw that the crematorium trees were in full leaf. Long-tailed titmice roved through the canopies, hyperactive and frail, their tails like emery boards glued onto cotton reel bodies, making sharp little contact calls that sounded like the kiss and clack of needles. Like the contents of Grandma's knitting box come alive. She would have smiled to see them. She loved birds, and always put food out in her back garden, treading round the puddles in her dressing gown and slippers. She loved music, too. And children. She loved all pointless and incorruptible things.

Afterwards there was the awkward English sandwich reception in a long unheated hall in Eardlem. Amber tea plaited out of runny-nosed aluminium urns and the coronation chicken had raisins in it, like we were still in the 1980s. The hall is right by the motte of the Norman castle, where my family have so often walked. There's a little stream up there from which I used to fetch watercress with my uncle Jack, Grandma's brother. In the 1980s the sky was full of swallows and house martins who used mud from this same little stream to mould their nests. They streamed over the hills in the wind, and chattered to each other as they worked individually, in couples and communally to build homes for themselves in an annual ritual I expect no one thought would ever end.

2

After the funeral we returned home and everyday life resumed as though nothing had happened. I was richly occupied again with family, my job, immediate duties and immediate pleasures. But in the weeks that followed I was dogged by unease. By day I was anxious without apparent cause, and each night, after lying awake for hours, I was outcast on a small, oarless boat over what I sensed was a depthless darkness, on a lake or at sea, sometimes glimpsing, sometimes only feeling how just below the surface vast creatures heaved and strove, black dreamwater slopping off their smooth, arced backs. Some nights I would dive in, wishing to get close to them, but they accelerated always beyond my sight. Then I was back in the boat, quite dry. Yet the next night the animals would return, joggling the boat with black bow waves and trailing, when they departed, long suggestive wakes. Plainly, something was trying to work its way up, make itself known; something I conjectured had to do with the loss of Grandma but belonged also to a larger and more elusive disturbance. But I couldn't work it out, couldn't even see the shape of it.

As has happened so often in my life, I was helped through confusion by something I read. It was an aphorism of the Scottish poet, gardener and philosopher Ian Hamilton Finlay, a strange, driven man, full of love but cussed to the world, a self-conscious exile in his own country and century, who had lately come to fascinate me. Severely agoraphobic, Finlay, with his wife Sue, had in the second half of his life bought seven acres of moorland in the Pentland Hills and over thirty years transformed it by hand into a neoclassical garden of trees, ponds, sculptures and heroic inscriptions in stone. When a commentator carelessly described the garden as a retreat, Finlay countered that it was in fact an attack: an attack on the loss of order and grandeur in contemporary life.

But the quotation from Finlay that stayed with me is as follows:

It is the case with gardens as with societies: some things require to be *fixed* so that others may be *placed*.

This aphorism had already preoccupied me for weeks, but on my return to Swansea from a trip to Little Sparta, Finlay's moorland garden, it seemed to ground itself with new force in the truth of my circumstances. I felt that I now understood its practical value, which for me had nothing to do with gardening, but seemed to identify very accurately what I felt to be wrong with myself. Finlay's words enabled me to understand that in losing Grandma and Eardlem I had been bereaved of precisely a fixed point of orientation. As a result I myself had become displaced and adrift, without coordinates or anything to steer by save the cryptic suggestions of the dream-beasts. Or at least this is how I had felt since the funeral, but now this metaphor of Finlay's advertised itself as a kind of foothold and starting point to explore what was troubling me.

So I began to explore, and it was intimidating. Slowly and staccato, throughout that late autumn and early winter of 2019, I was brought to realize that in fact this process of displacement had been going on for many years, with the loss of Grandma and Eardlem only the snapping of the final rope in a long, apparently inexorable unmooring. And as I began somewhat reluctantly to examine, as it were, these frayed ends I'd been left holding, I found that they resembled in sum a single immense and tangled clew of problems, though all involving different kinds of loss between which I'd never before reasoned a connection. None of this came to me clearly. There was no question of a great eureka. In my waking hours there was barely a moment. Blatant mid-life crisis was a luxury I couldn't afford. But Finlay's axiom was the bright hook that slowly, nocturnally, drew up the aquatic animals of my dreaming whose function, I was now certain, was to shunt me from lostness towards some kind of identity or purpose.

Meanwhile, it was spring again, that strangest spring of the first pandemic. I lost my job, was bedridden with Covid, got a publishing deal and wrote a book about the birds I could see and hear around me in Swansea. When the schools reopened, the photographer came in to take the belated annual portraits. As we compared this year's with the previous year's photos, we exclaimed with parental pride but also wondered aloud at how the children's faces were changing, their features forever taking on fresh resemblances, to my wife or me, our parents, uncles and aunts, grandparents. And most evenings between our son's bedtime and midnight I sat abstractedly in the study while Grandma and Grandad looked down at me from a photograph nailed to the wall above my desk. They are standing in the back garden of the house at Eardlem, but the washing line goes right through Grandad's head. The photograph is so bad that only I could have taken it.

You hear that good writers keep systematic notebooks of their daily impressions as records of experience later to be trans-formed into art. With me, the likelihood of writing seems

inversely related to the number of pretty notebooks I buy. But from my twenties I sometimes wrote down dreams that affected me powerfully, and I knew that if I looked through my old notebooks I would find dated entries concerning the dream-beasts. They would be few, but at least something, a place to start. So one evening in my study, as a deep-red moon rose over Swansea Bay, I fetched from the cupboard fifteen or so notebooks and pads of different colours and sizes. I stacked them next to my chair and over the next two hours pored through them slowly in solipsistic fascination. I found that uneasy dreams of water went back a long way. The earliest entry was from 2003, when I had been living in York, very close to the banks of the River Ouse:

6 a.m. Heavy fatigue and the thick residue of dreams. I leaped from a bridge into the cold brown Ouse, and sank deep into the water, where I received a phone call from my mother. I couldn't make out what she wanted, so hung up. I thought I was rising, but felt my feet hit the river bed. I kicked away from it, pushing back to the surface, and woke when my head emerged from the water.

There were also many animals in the dreams – chimeras and demons as well as more familiar forms. But amphibians and reptiles were the most common, as in this one from 2012, which at first I thought irrelevant to my search.

On or around the night of 20th March I dreamed that I found a painted bowl of Roman porcelain in a marsh, and that it contained various big-eyed unfamiliar amphibians, slimy and cool to the touch, about the size and texture of pelmeni [pelmeni are Russian ravioli]. The animals looked exposed and vulnerable in the bowl, and I was still deciding whether to sink it back into the bog-water or take it home when I awoke.

I suppose I had always been in haste to record the dreams before I forgot them. At any rate, I seem to have reached for whichever notebook was nearest to hand, since records from the same year were often spread over two or three volumes. I enjoyed revisiting the dreams so much that it was often necessary to remind myself that I wasn't reading for pleasure but in search of a pattern. But it was only as I began to assemble the entries from 2017 that I began to think I had found one. The entries began in early June of that year, and three in particular struck me as related:

The maelstrom, night 2nd–3rd June: Near darkness, through which becomes visible a huge and fissured slab of coastal rock, wet and glistening black. A ship has run aground but all the men have made it onto the rock. From above and slightly shakily I see them, as though through a television camera on a circling helicopter, make their way slowly across the rock, bodies taut to keep foothold on the uneven surface in a strong wind. I know the wind is strong because I can now see a gigantic crater of violent, raging seawater in the middle of the rock. It is a maelstrom that the sea has made. The line of men is picking its way carefully around the rim of the maelstrom and then slowly away, but one man seems unable to leave the edge. As though drunk, he teeters on the lip of the crater, a minuscule figure in a vast sunless land-scape. One or two of the other men turn back to help him, try to lead him away from the crater by the arm while they shout, as I somehow know, words of exhortation through the gale. Now some information comes into my mind, as though the scene were being narrated: a voiceover without a voice. I am told that there seems nothing wrong with the man; his shipmates cannot under-stand why he can't walk away from the crater, and perhaps he can't understand it himself. The voiceover stops, and for a short while longer I see the man, a tiny, hunched figure, like a wasp on the rim of a beer glass. Then I can't see him any more. The mael-strom sucks and seethes. I can only guess that the man is lost.

30th August. All I can recall of a long, complex dream was my trying to feed a lizard some orangish mush from a silver tea-spoon. The lizard was really a magician who had been reduced to this form by the effort of protecting me and others from dark powers. I pushed the spoon into his slightly open mouth but the food fell again from his lips. The lizard's face is still vivid to me:

thin, grey, wrinkled, showing great suffering, infinite resignation in its wise, tired eye and the grim set of its mouth.

Early morning of 2nd September. Aboard an old-fashioned ship. There was a grey creature like a plesiosaur in the water under the ship, and we were feeding it. It would swim to the surface of the sea to take our food. In the next scene, both the plesiosaur-creature and one of our crew had been captured and mistreated by cruel men. The animal had been confined to a small pool where it could barely swim. It had grown thin and weak from this treatment, and the man was haggard too. When the wicked men let them go, our crew-mate stood there limply with the equally flaccid animal draped around his neck and across his shoulders, the dream having shrunk the animal for the purposes of showing me this image. Both man and animal survived, however, and we began feeding them to restore them to health. The plesiosaur resumed its former position alongside our boat and we lowered food to it as before until it began to recover.

It was the themes of threat, nourishment and anxious care in these last two fragments that led me to connect them with the dream about the pale amphibians in the Roman bowl from five years earlier. But it took longer than it should have for me to realize that in each case the timing of these dreams corresponded to my wife's pregnancies with our two younger children. At the second scan of Thomas, in 2017, potential abnormalities were detected in his growing brain, and I attributed the greater frequency and intensity of anxiety dreams that summer to my concern for him.

It seemed very plausible that the dreams of nourishment partly concerned my hopes and fears for my unborn children. Yet if that were all there was to it, how to explain the continued presence and increasing frequency of the dream-beasts since 2017? That year had been significant for at least two other reasons: it was when I had suffered a personal crisis, and also when we had moved from England to Wales, a decision that the crisis had partly occasioned. Although much about the crisis remained obscure, it had involved a loss of faith in language, in a sense of purpose, of hope and belonging, and it had taken a lot of effort and a change of home and environment to recover from the worst of its effects. In recent years I had allowed myself to think I was clear of it, and though I knew this wasn't really so, I had been mostly able to ignore it. The dream creatures had never gone away, but in the months before Grandma's death they had visited me seldom, and troubled me less. Now something about her loss and that of Eardlem had brought them back, drawn them up again from whatever abyss of the brain they belong in.

This was the basic but significant connection that Finlay's epigram had helped me drag to light. The disorientation I had been feeling these last months since the funeral might indeed have been provoked by the loss of Grandma and Eardlem, but it also went back much further and was fed by anxieties that I had long half-succeeded in burying. Now I knew that I couldn't avoid them any more. But insofar as what troubled me went beyond my grief for Grandma, I found that my efforts to think things through were meeting a stubborn inner resistance. The greater my effort to identify deeper causes, the more I suspected my mind of working against me. My enquiring will just separated itself from the problem like oil from water, and to my own surprise I would find myself on YouTube or simply gazing out of the study window to the almost invisible line where the pale-grey ocean meets the pale-grey sky. Still, I knew, somewhere, what this was really all about, or at least where my confrontation with it should begin.

3

On a train between Bristol and Bath, in the spring of 2017, my mind cracked. For months I had felt an unnatural exhaustion that in moments of clarity I'd already assumed to be the front for some swelling, anonymous dread, but closer to the surface lay obvious material factors that I could at first pass off as causes. My partner and I were both working full time on insecure contracts, without holiday or sick pay, while trying to look after two children and a third on the way. I had also recently been forced to recognize that my job was making me ill. I was a university teacher of study skills, and my days and most evenings were spent skimming over essays and reports to identify problems with the writing and suggest fixes, so that students would gain confidence and pass their courses. Almost all the students were from overseas, studying subjects like management and accountancy. Their parents had paid tens of thousands to send them here so that they could benefit from the twilight prestige of a British degree and enter the business world at a lucrative level. With the rarest exceptions these students were pleasant, courteous and attentive, yet it troubled me that none of them seemed to question the motives or implied ethics of the system which assured them of this advantage. In two or three years these students would be middle- or high-ranking functionaries in the international financial and business culture, and this was for them no more than they had paid for. The few home students I taught were also overwhelmingly incurious about the wider purpose and value of what they were studying beyond its utility in landing them a Masters degree and a well-paid job. That some organizations and their human resources required to be managed, and that it was they who would do the managing, was taken as the natural way of things.

I was troubled by what seemed the evident link between the commodification of learning and the intellectual passivity of these otherwise delightful young people, and by my own role as an abettor of the system. But this was only one face of a greater anxiety. Every day the serious media reported the accelerating climate crisis. Like warning signs beside a motorway, tipping-points were left behind almost as soon as they were acknowledged. The world seemed unable to wean itself off capital accumulation and the exploitation that drives it, and it felt like nothing could be done. If there was any hope, then we were told it lay with the generations now coming to adulthood. Yet each academic year I helped feed hundreds of polite, hardworking, clever young people into the world of globalized corporate finance that was pushing everything I loved over a cliff.

The university campus was the concrete pate of a hill tonsured with remnants of old forest. In gaps between classes I would walk among the trees and try to make sense of where I was and what I was doing there. At any other time in my life before then, a walk in the woods might have been enough to replenish me. Since early childhood I had found rest and delight in the natural world, but now I was simultaneously so busy and so unfocused that I registered my surroundings dully, as though through a smeared screen. If a woodpecker called from the trees or a raven grunted overhead, I would mark it but without enthusiasm. In the part of my mind these independent lives would usually relieve, there ran instead a ceaseless involuntary soundtrack of advertising jingles, drum fills, song lyrics on repeat. I dimly understood that I was a bit sick, and that the sickness was bound up both with my busyness and the depleted life of the natural and cultural words. To my utter distress, I now found that the old sources of comfort were instead the sites of my greatest anxiety.

The sickness was also manifest in an exhaustion with language, which had always been the other of my soul's great joys. In what I now believe was a half-conscious strategy not to look inside myself, I had lately begun to read, compulsively and without discrimination or real interest, whatever kind of message came my way. I was trying to suppress an inner voice with a constant stream of external stimuli. And I was unable to switch off: I feasted on promotional spew and planning applications tagged to lampposts, looking constantly for anagrams, palindromes, puns. I'd sometimes catch myself on the walk through the streets of Bath hungrily forming words from the letters on car numberplates, or trying to eavesdrop on conversations. But even if I found a vacant classroom and sat awhile in silence there was no relief from the words that whirled around my mind in lifeless animation, the way that dust and leaves are spun in mini cyclones when they are boxed in by buildings and cornered by concrete and glass.

It happened in an overcrowded and airless carriage. I can't remember the time of day or which way the train was going. I had my head down near my phone. I swiped away from something trivial and started to read about the vicious heatwave then affecting Australia and almost the whole of Southern Asia. There were record numbers of bushfires. Animals were unable to escape and were dying in thousands. Peoples' homes were alight. It was Australia but I knew it could have been anywhere, and would soon be everywhere. I understood that the world had already started to burn. I read the story, looked at the pictures of people receiving water and medical aid, then looked up and out of the window at the blurred housing estates and identical ryegrass fields. And it was then that I felt a jolt and a black crack in my brain. I think I knew straightaway what had happened, or rather, what kind of thing, but it wasn't a knowledge I could articulate. Now, at seven years' distance, I recognize it as the moment that disenchantment struck me. I lost faith in what I was doing in the context of a new certainty about the dying world, while on a train between two places to which I felt no connection at all.

I can say all this quite easily now, but at the time my whole psyche went to work to protect me. My mind opted out, chose not to understand, and so my body bore the brunt. That same week I had to cancel a lesson I was giving midway through, because I wasn't breathing properly and felt I was going to be sick. There was a pressure in my temples as though a clamp was tightening around my head. I was signed off for a few weeks, but there was little respite at home. My brain was still full of noise and I was exhausted all the time, which put extra pressure on my partner to care for our children. My breathing was in an absolute state. I would alternate between bouts of fast, shallow panting and then somehow neglect to breathe at all until I took a huge reflexive gasp and it began all over again. Most evenings I hadn't enough breath to read the children a bedtime story.

Week after week I put off going for a walk in the woods near where we rented, despite understanding that part of what had struck me was caused by a lack of aloneness, and by what was then starting to be called 'burnout'. Yes, a walk in the woods! Just to be alone on the soil with nothing to read and no one to 'read' me and no one to be offended if I just sit on the ground for ten minutes with my eyes closed, to feel the clamp loosen, and curiosity and spontaneity return. I couldn't have said why I didn't take that option, though I know now.

It was because when I looked quickly, wincingly, at the crack that had appeared in me, and glanced at where its dark lines ran, I understood on a deep level that this was not merely a case of needing a break. Since childhood, my two refuges in times of stress had been language and contact with the natural world. Now that language was making me ill and the world outside the train, just beyond the horizon, was withering, lessening, burning, what recourse was there? I grasped negatively, by deprivation, that what I had always valued so highly in the natural world was its purity. There were many elements to this purity, all of which were sullied. In the most literal sense, I had believed – needed to believe – that the world was physically clean. I was disturbed by pollution of course, but had been able to persuade myself that instances of pollution were accidental, limited and reversible. Now though, when I sought mental relief from the word-blizzard by imagining a vast blue ocean, all I could think about were the too warm, acid waters, and the shellfish ingesting plastics. At home I had a coffee-table book of Dutch landscape art. I opened it and looked at a painting called 'Grainfields', by van Ruisdael, a beautiful landscape under a vast sky, and all I could think was that back then the clouds he painted had been clean, clean, clean. There was nowhere to go.

In a poem I had memorized at school, 'the crack in the teacup opens / a lane to the land of the dead'. I had felt the power of these lines for years, but had not understood them. It was precisely this bleak connection across scales that I was suddenly aware of, not abstractly but internally. Newly visible despair lines traced personal unhappiness to a grubby apocalypse and the exploitation and neglect that ultimately feed both. I came to this awareness only gradually, but it didn't need to manifest fully for me to sense that it threatened my hope – and not only in the future but also, strangely, my confidence in the past. It was obvious, of course, why the devastation of the Earth should cause me to lose hope in the future – which I believe for most parents is thought of first as the children's future, not ours – but for the first time in the aftermath of that grim train journey I sensed that my past, too, had been taken away, or rather that the innocence, purity and hope I had felt assured of in the happiness of my childhood had always, even then, been unfounded.

One afternoon in the summer of 1986, when I was ten years old, I followed my Dad down to the garage to fetch out the two wooden trestle tables that we used for spreading paste onto the back of wallpaper. We dragged them into the sunlight of the front garden and Dad showed me how to lie them flat on their backs before unfolding their legs. They resembled huge, stiff-legged insects with creaky joints, and setting them upright caused them to leak real spiders of all sizes, from which my sister and I fled and watched from an appalled distance until they had reached the shaded margins of the lawn. Then, when we'd wiped the grime and webs from the tabletops, we all helped bring out the unwanted toys, homemade jam tarts and chocolate cornflake cakes we were to sell. We were raising money for the World Wildlife Fund. We would save the panda; we would save the whale.

We'd flyered the cul-de-sac the previous day and our small front garden was visited by a steady stream of neighbours. Two hours later it was all over and sparrows flew down from the cherry tree for the cake crumbs brushed off the trestles. At the end of the day we stacked the coins by denomination in unsteady piles, straightened them carefully between index and thumb and gave them to Dad, who signed a cheque to the WWF with the real ink pen he used for work. I wrote a letter to go with it, and the next morning we dropped the envelope into the pillar-box on the main road.

Then as now, this probably wasn't a common thing for children to do, but we knew that it happened sometimes, because I was in the Young Ornithologists' Club and received their magazine through the post, where I read accounts of similar sales. By ten my other childhood interests had fallen away, and reading and birdwatching were what occupied me most. The interest transferred to my parents, and soon we bought a bird table and began to visit the local nature reserve, me with the metal badge of the YHA constantly needing to be re-pinned through my thick duffle coat. Slowly, by regular and loving looking, I internalized the shapes and calls and manners of the birds. And the birds and their haunts became part of my wider education about the world, running parallel to but deeper than the formal education I was receiving at school. Partly it was an education in particulars. I believe that it was through observing birds that I extended my perception of colour and first experienced the inadequacy of my felt-tips to approximate, say, the warm pink brick of a kestrel's back or the subtleties of brown on a snipe's wings and breast.

Thirty years later, in the summer of 2017, the crack in my mind still new, I read backwards to 1986. I learned that in the December of that year, four months after our front-garden sale, the scientist Carl Sagan testified before the US Congress on the dangers of global warming. Sagan acknowledged that on a small scale human beings had probably been altering the climate for a long time, but now 'The power of human beings to affect and control and change the environment is growing as our technology grows, and at present time we clearly have reached the stage where we are capable (both intentionally and inadvertently) to make significant changes in the global climate and in the global ecosystem.' It's entirely possible that even as Sagan was speaking, my dad and I were sitting in a bird hide, sipping tea from flasks, our numb fingers slowly prising sandwiches from tinfoil, reluctant to turn away from the slit in the wood into which poured the fading winter light of the marsh. Teal flew in and splashed down, water rails crept timidly from the reeds. We sat in silent camaraderie, gaze turned outwards at the independent life of the marsh and lake, a world in which human emotions and ego held no significance. Dad was then the age that I've reached now. Naturally, I never gave a thought to one day having children of my own. Sagan continued, 'If you don't worry about it now, it's too late later on. We are passing down extremely grave problems for our children, when the time to solve the problems is now.'

In 2024 the truth of what Sagan said is inescapable, or rather it can only be escaped by escaping from truth altogether. And we who were born and grew to maturity in the middle years of the twentieth century realize that all the time we played and laughed and grew we were being outpaced by a wave of destruction of our species' own making. By now the story is familiar. I think to most people it is honestly pretty boring. But the book lies open, and anyone who is up to it can read about the postwar consumer boom, the enforced privatizations, the financialization of everything, including the water and the earth itself, from the late 1970s onwards.

I had ceased to cope with all this in 2017, and though I had succeeded for a while in papering it over, the damage had never been repaired. Now, three years later, the loss of Grandma and Eardlem made further concealment impossible. I often still caught myself trying to avoid its implications, but the dream-beasts told me that I was stalling and often only pretending to look, afraid to investigate too closely in dread of what I might discover about the extent of my lostness but also about how this was related to the loss of the world itself. Thirty years separated my own childhood from those of my children, but into those thirty years had been poured many centuries' worth of destruction. And measuring from the childhood of my parents, more destruction had happened within those sixty years than in millennia preceding it.

Now that I was finally being made to confront it, the neglect of the sources of life was apparent every day, and all around me. Everything on these islands speaks of homelessness and the want of care. Greed, exploitation, willed blindness were the names of a wave washing away everything that had previously been humane, vernacular, rooted. The wave is also called 'market forces', a bland pseudonym so vague that the mind can't even grasp it, let alone oppose it. But like any deity it manifests concretely in its effects. Marketization is being unable to rent or buy a home, it is the need to commute, it is a shiny-fronted squalid procession of bookmakers' and vape shops and it is the reason you don't receive sick pay when you haven't the breath to read to your children. Like a wave it is vast, liquid, ungraspable. Like a wave it bears along at a frightening lick everything it has smashed and slopped away, people and things alike. Looking around now, I could see only planks and fragments of the natural and cultural abundance that my parents' generation had inherited.

Planks and fragments. I thought these words and wrote them down. A few days later, back in the study overlooking Swansea

Bay, and remembering Eardlem, I related them for the first time to certain physical objects that I had inherited from my grandparents' house. To that point I had not thought about these objects as anything but inanimate *stuff*. I'd have laughed if you'd said they could help me. But the thought that they and I were caught up in the same wave shifted my perspective a little, and caused me to look at them differently, with something like sympathy. Weren't they every bit as bereft of belonging as I felt myself to be? Weren't they and I, as the slogan goes, 'in it together'.

I had already begun to wonder whether the web of fissures that had riven my mind, the crack in the teacup that connected my personal suffering to cultural and planetary death, could be looked at not only as a threat to my health and sanity but also and at the same time as potentially, albeit distantly, *useful*. To be sure, I was still painfully lost inside this riddle of cracks, but by now I also had some perspective on it, could see it sometimes almost from above. And from this more detached perspective it could be made to resemble, I thought, a sort of labyrinth or map. For the first time, then, it occurred to me that the mass of loose ends I'd been left holding when I'd been unmoored from Grandma and Eardlem could actually help me find a way through this maze. The problem was where to start. It was in this context that I had begun to visualize personal and global calamity as a wave that washed everything away – a wave in which I myself was a fragment, but not the only one. I enjoyed the dark humour, then, of imagining myself as part of a *community* of fragments. Yet wasn't it true? So I began to look around me at what else had been washed up, to see if there was anything that could, maybe, be put to practical use, that could act as a clue. At this stage I could not have guessed that the path to recovery would lead to the homes of my parents and to a reckoning with Eardlem itself, yet also beyond, to the enchanted ground of friends old and new. I did not yet know how to bring the loose ends together – how, to put it baldly, to find continued value in a front-garden cake sale while the world was dying. All I knew for now, when I thought harder about what had happened to my grandparents' house in Eardlem, and looked around at what had been salvaged from it, was that I was after all not entirely alone.

4

When a home is struck by its final death and leaves the protective atmosphere of a family, it suffers a silent explosion that scatters the objects once held close. Some are flung out very far from reliable care, to charity shops, clearance dealers, landfill. Such objects become unfamiliar. They grow cold, become mere bric-a-brac and debris, lose even the power to haunt. But if objects should stay within the family, they seem to remember something of their old purposefulness.

With the loss of my grandparents' house in Eardlem, certain objects, 'came down' to me. That is, as it seemed for a long while afterwards, they had descended from a lost but meaningful past to a diminished and disoriented present. There was no room in our house for extra furniture, but I chose from the more portable stuff an ornamented fire screen that wobbles on wooden claws; a colourful blanket knitted by my Aunty May, like a rose garden in cobbled wool; an aluminium colander and a cord-handled vegetable peeler that with its banded torso and hangdog mien suggested a miniature armadillo. In the immediate aftermath of Grandma's death, and ever since, I now recognized that these objects had offered succour in the face of my grief and confusion, as fellow survivors of the loss.

In an essay of 1922, a young resident of St Petersburg, the writer Osip Mandelstam, thinks hard about the ideal relationship between human beings and objects, a relationship he calls

'Hellenism': 'Hellenism is an earthenware pot, oven tongs, a milk jug, kitchen utensils, dishes; it is anything which surrounds the body. Hellenism is the warmth of the hearth experienced as something sacred; it is anything which imparts some of the external world to man.' Even beyond this, though, it is 'the transformation of impersonal objects into domestic utensils, and the humanizing and warming of the surrounding world' when objects are 'brought into man's sacred circle'.

I doubt that anyone nowadays believes in 'man's sacred circle'. Our sense of ourselves has changed and we are too much aware of human evil. But still, when Mandelstam says that 'man' can experience his/her relationship with objects as sacred, this is surely true to our ordinary experience, even if we bridle at that word 'sacred'. Organized religions have their holy objects, but isn't this just a shrewd institutional appropriation of a basic, universal and thoroughly 'pagan' reverence for inanimate things in which we sense a continuity of human care? It really might be anything: a drystone wall, a shovel, a pair of shoes, a leather watch strap, a paperweight – even an ordinary if armadillo-like vegetable peeler, recently exiled from a magnetic utensil rack in an unremarkable home in the north Midlands.

A century before Mandelstam's essay, another sensitive young man went on a walking tour in the Harz Mountains, where he received hospitality in remote villages. Heinrich Heine was a brilliant and ironic metropolitan sophisticate, but his experience in the mountains drew from him a different tone, one of humility and respect for the people who gave him shelter. He writes that,

> Although the life these people lead may seem calm and immobile, it is nevertheless a genuine, living life. The ancient, tremulous woman who was sitting beside the stove opposite the big

cupboard may have sat there for a quarter of a century, and her thoughts and feelings are closely interwoven with every corner of the stove and every carving on the cupboard. And the stove and cupboard are alive, for part of a human soul has entered into them.

Heine goes on to claim that this long and mutually dependent cohabitation of humans and their sacred objects produced and explains the apparent absurdities of German fairy tales,

which [are] characterized by the presence not only of animals and plants, but even of supposedly inanimate objects as speakers and actors . . . A needle and a pin leave the tailors' hostel and lose their way in the dark; a piece of straw and a lump of coal try to cross the river and are drowned . . . even drops of blood begin to speak, uttering dark and fearful words of concern and compassion.

Heine writes that the 'inner lives' of objects and animals were formerly revealed to those who live alongside them. Now, however,

our furnishings are of little interest to us, for either they are new, or else they are Hans's today and Isaac's tomorrow. Even our clothes are alien to us: we scarcely know how many buttons there are on the coat we are wearing at this moment; we change our garments so often that none of them retains any connection with the history of our minds and our bodies.

I must have read these passages dozens of times, but on every rereading I am surprised again that an alienation from objects I'd associated with the late twentieth century should already have been apparent to Heine early in the nineteenth. I still think that before industrialization our relationship with objects would necessarily have been less casual, more careful. In every human society we know of, stretching outwards into space and backwards beyond history into the youth of our species, as attested in writing and art and in the archaeological record of troves and exhumations, certain objects have always been chosen as our companions not only through life but also into the grave or onto the pyre.

As well as sobering us with knowledge that the throwaway society began earlier than we usually suppose, Heine's comment also highlights an ethical crux, basic in human nature, which in every generation and individual obliges a choice between whether to exploit and commodify or whether to care. Considering our relationship to objects in this way – I mean as implying a moral choice – itself restores our agency and therefore also our responsibility. That we live among, and are complicit in, extraordinarily wasteful and careless habits of thought and production in no way obliges us to be passive or excuses a lack of care. Even if you believe (as I do) that there is some qualitative or essential difference between a hand-carved wooden toy made by a relative and its plastic equivalent mass-produced in a factory on the other side of the world, if the latter is kept and loved and thereby brought into 'man's sacred circle', then the impersonal, transactional network of capitalism is minutely humanized, the cold world slightly warmed and something anonymous made to belong.

I enjoyed recognizing and then rereading the fairy tales that Heine referenced. In our family the notion that objects are in a sense alive and can be regarded as people is normal. We all, or certainly my mother, sister and I, habitually address ourselves to recalcitrant light fittings, overboiling coffee pots or refusenik thumbtacks without discrimination or embarrassment. Though we are grown-up people we never seem to have been persuaded out of this instinctive, affectionate animism. Once I began to consider the objects from the Eardlem house, my fellow exiles, with affection and love, to notice them more, to pat them as I passed by or bring them with me in the evening to rest upon my desk, it seemed to me that the house and Grandma were drawn closer. I actively sought them out and I felt better for it, perhaps even more grounded.

This feeling of comfort wasn't constant, or underwritten by any guarantee. Even as the peeler and the other objects offered nourishment, they also advertised their fragility. They were after all fragments of a life passed, and this I never forgot. Like wreckage from a ship gone down they had been left bobbing, unintegrated, on life's surface, bereft of the place where they had been purposeful in the family ecosystem centred on Grandma. But though they were exiled, I could also now see that the objects were not void of meaning. They were not mere debris, and when I wondered why this should be so, I was surprised that such an obvious answer should have come to me so slowly: it was because I still valued them. That was the first time I understood that objects need us too, and either suffer in our neglect or thrive in our care. And this little revelation felt to me like it could be the first step towards regaining some orientation in my life. The vegetable peeler and its confederates had belonged in a past that was gone. But what if the most important thing wasn't the inevitable loss of the past, but that the objects should be given another context for belonging? Rooted meaningfully but not limitingly in the past, they were now fellow travellers with me into the future, and my meaning was bound up with theirs.

In another, different folk tale I'd recently read to my daughter, three witches make themselves small and straddle twigs before shooting up the chimney with the sparks and out into the world with a wheesh. The tale makes no suggestion that the twigs are in any sense magical, 'have powers', until the witches pick them up; yet equally, the witches cannot fly without them. Perhaps they would not even *be* witches and enjoy these improbable flights were it not for their special relationship with these otherwise quite ordinary twigs. Yes, in the tale everything seems to depend on this relationship, and the trust it implies.

The next evening – it must have been about nine o'clock – in playful earnest, I closed my hand around Grandma's vegetable peeler, with which for almost a century, scraping deftly backwards, she had planed away the mottled skin and sculpted the sallow and sweet-smelling flanks of numberless spuds. I shut my eyes and gripped the peeler, imagining my hands, imagining hers. I gripped it until I could believe that we shared the same warmth. A south-westerly was whining at my study window and briny rain spattered the pane. I ignored it, kept my eyes closed, thought of Eardlem and Grandma. I concentrated more fiercely, clutched harder, and after a couple of false starts there was this motionless acceleration and we really were off, the peeler and I, like a spark shooting up and backwards into darkness, with a fixed point of light just visible at the other end.

I am in her kitchen. Her slippers slap and scuff on the quarry tiles as she crosses to fill a bowl of water where the potatoes will soak. By the light pouring in through the rain-beaded window it must be just gone noon. Now she stands at the cooker and plants a hissing blue lotus beneath the chip pan. When I was tall and trusted enough I used to love looking over the lip of the pan at the small bubbles of golden oil clinging or crawling along the goldening discs. Behind her is the sink with two blue rubber gloves flopped on the draining board and the row of rubber-flanged holes, like the anuses of cats, into which we must poke the corners of tea towels. And beyond the sink and the silver raindrops is the back garden, and beyond the garden a single swallow plies above the fields that rise to the reservoir-capped hill. Grandma is singing as she works, and now Mum joins her as she enters through the back door in a cool green gust of cut grass.

It could have been 'Mairzy Doats', or 'Chattanooga Choo Choo', but today it is an aria of Puccini. I am not in the kitchen now but hear it through the open door leading from the back room, where I sit sweeping plastic Scrabble tiles into their green drawstring bag so the table can be set for dinner. The doorframe is filled with steam, and now Grandma emerges from it at the threshold, animated and inspired. 'Don't you know this one!' She is full of the music's grandeur. Mum appears beside her, and they hum and laa and Grandma waves the gravy ladle like a baton through the clouds of vegetable steam and the oven's roasted exhalations. They are on the stage at La Scala and, no, *scusa*, they don't know Italian, but what matters is the emotion of the thing. I watch them and smile, and the tiles stop plinking into the bag and fall instead onto the carpet.

I quickly became adept at these flights into the past, using the peeler much as a shaman uses feather and drum. After all the mental agitation of the last year, and the great long repression that had suffocated me before, it was sheer relief simply to remember for remembrance's sake, and to feel close to Grandma and Eardlem again, and to my own childhood when the world had seemed less troubled. In quiet moments, when the children were at school and I could work from home, I found my way into reveries where I would revisit the Eardlem house one room at a time, and I could almost convince myself that I was really there, a ghost from the future.

Along the narrow hall was the front room. This was the lair of Uncle Jack, who had come to live with Grandma and Grandad for a few days in 1962 and somehow never left. My sister and I were a little reluctant to use the room while Jack was in there, though I would sometimes kneel by his armchair and squint with him through the stinking wisps of grey and yellow cigarette smoke at the cowboys and 'Indians' on the small black-and-white TV. There was in those days a permanent smog over the Sierra Nevada. The front room received little sunlight, and because it was always cold the gas fire was often lit. When Jack left for a walk along the old colliery railway line, sometimes with an easel and palette tilting in his armpit, my sister and I would relax into the room, drawn mostly by the fire itself, which in time we were permitted to light, though it had a truculent ignition that yielded only to an expert simultaneous depress and twist of its stiff plastic dial. There was little danger because the flames were behind bars, but the fire was a novelty to us who at home had to make do with radiators, so we maximized what peril there was by holding our faces as close to the heat as we could bear. The mantel above the fire was of fake marble, and among its denizens I remember particularly a wickerwork owl with a removable head and red eyes that would have been completely unremarkable had I not been reading during those years Arthur C. Clarke's stories of the paranormal, featuring the horrible cryptid known as the Mawnan Owlman.

This book was one of the very few that interested us on our grandparents' shelves. There was a mid-century compendium of 'classic' children's tales, but the retellings were stilted and the illustrations washy and twee, so I spent more time with the Times Dictionary, which was brought out regularly for crossword duty and as the arbiter of our disputes over Scrabble. But my greatest sources of pleasure, in the endless torpor of those Sunday afternoons when the adults cooked or napped, were the encyclopedias – the multiple illustrated volumes of the Reader's Digest Encyclopedia but also the more portable Pears Cyclopedia. Lying on the carpet, flat-out before the fire, my curiosity would slake itself in these colossi of cultured information and their deft line illustrations – of wild asses of the Eurasian steppe, ladies' fashions of the fin de siècle and bamboo-hatted Malay fisherman carefully lowering sketchy wicker fish traps into roughly indicated water.

The intangible, nonfungible pleasure of browsing those illustrated dictionaries and encyclopedias, seeded long ago in my grandparents' house in Eardlem, has never left me. And I feel a huge, diffuse gratitude that I was left in peace to wander those lively rows of words and images, next to which the internet is nothing but a sleazy boutique. Now as then, to open a good illustrated dictionary is to happen upon a marketplace whose joy lies in random encounters and surprising, disinterested associations. Online dictionaries can never be dipped into with true innocence, since you first need to type in the term you are looking for. But what if you are not looking for anything beyond the pleasure of sonic and semantic association? As any wanderer of marketplaces, flea markets and old-style charity shops knows, the joy is that you're looking for nothing and everything at the same time. Nearly twenty years after I bought it in Moscow, abandoning most of my clothes at the airport's check-in desk to offset its weight, my 1961 Merriam-Webster illustrated dictionary is suffering with age and continuous use. Gigantic on my desk, like a stranded whale it has collapsed under its own mass and slumped and separated into three still vast slabs of barely bound paper, rippled like baleen. Divine any slab at random and you will find wonders: *hebdomad (n): a group of seven*, and again *pishogue (n): a wise saw or aphorism*. Wonderful! I have been doing this for years, and by now have an alternative ABC primer beginning '*abele, breloque, catafalque*'

Even at nine years old, as I flipped through Grandma and Grandad's encyclopedias on the ash-infused carpet of Uncle Jack's room, I knew full well that I needed these words in my life. And I hope that children still do this, for without curious readers to visit it, the marketplace of words will fall silent. It will be the silence of a high-end high street after the shutters have come down, a street whose only function is to sell you things. This, finally, is the difference between a dictionary and the internet: that the first is deciduous, and garrulous with chance meetings, resembling a Spanish town at dusk where the plazas and their radiating lanes are full of people conversing and flirting, and children shrieking around the fountains; but the internet is as sterile as the centres of London or Birmingham when trading hours are over: empty, gated, locked down and silent when there is nothing to be touted and no profit to be made.

The gas fire was flanked by twin porcelain tortoises whose shells lifted off so that the bases could be used as ashtrays. Perhaps they were thought too good for this purpose, because as I recall Uncle Jack only ever used a standing ashtray of fluted metal. Excused from practical duty, the tortoises were free to roam, grunting, around the carpet and up the plush flanks of the sofas, piloted between our thumbs and forefingers with much helpless giggling. Some objects, like some people, possess a

greater gravitas, and we felt comfortable in animating and playing trivial games with the tortoises because they had no aura. Not
so the two or three wooden music boxes, some of them handmade
a few branches further up the family tree, which memory has
now compressed into one box. Pyrographed into its lid were clef-
shapes that you could trace with your finger, and it was wound
from below by a little metal bow. I think in later years one of us
must have twisted it too vigorously, and a colour of shame in
my memory leads me to suspect myself. Understandable, then,
that I prefer to recall the box in its happy pomp, when not only
the crank but also the little spring-loaded ballerina within the
box span like clockwork to the carillon of 'Wonderful Copenha-
gen'. Recalling this song, which many years later I incorporated
into the lullaby repertoire of my children, leads me to doubt that
it was in fact a ballerina. And the more I grope backwards the
more successfully I convince myself that the figure in the box was
actually a representation of Andersen's little mermaid, revolving
blissfully on her artificial rock until the last few notes of the song
stuttered into silence.

5

The objects I had inherited from my grandparents' house were an immediate comfort, but ever since I had first tentatively begun to relate the loss of Eardlem to a catalogue of wider crises, that crack in the teacup that linked my personal losses to those of culture and the planet, I had increasingly thought of them also as the first step in understanding and perhaps correcting what was wrong – that they could help me get a fix on myself. By now I was certain, besides, that it wasn't comfort I really needed, but fuller understanding. I didn't need cognitive behavioural therapy or a breather, I didn't need yoga or a holiday or a spa retreat. My feelings didn't need to be soothed or my symptoms 'managed'. And in that sense I dimly understood that I had to remain vulnerable, also, to what the objects *couldn't* do, and the feelings they couldn't assuage.

Yes, these objects and I belonged together as fellow castaways, and my flights to the past continued to help lessen the rupture between my present circumstances and the lost life of Eardlem. But they only addressed one aspect of the formidable problem that the dream-beasts were nosing me towards. And the beasts came very frequently now. One night we were on a Mediterranean clifftop overlooking the turquoise water of a cove; my daughter gripped my arm and pointed down to where two hammerhead sharks twisted in the shallows, their shadows twinning them on the barely submerged white sand. The next night my train was cancelled and I had to take a boat out onto a dark sea, accompanied invisibly all the way by huge submerged forms. On the third night I woke up and to the alarm of my wife actually laughed grimly aloud: for, seconds beforehand, I had simply drowned. I had swum up a pipe that promised to lead to the surface, but become stuck there, unable to exit in either direction.

Despite such occasional frights, I never seriously doubted my instinct that the dream-beasts were benevolent. Though I don't think it ever happened in a dream, by day I would sometimes imagine them nudging my small craft forwards, as in some sentimental story about helpful dolphins. My confidence in them, added to the assurance I had gained from my experimental mental flights back to Eardlem, allowed me to look less flinchingly at what had caused the crack in my mind that I had partially succeeded in avoiding but which still threatened to return in force, more than a year after Grandma's death.

Against the continuous temptation to retreat into the comfort of denial, I repeated to myself, over and again, the truth that the blow I had been dealt on that train between Bristol and Bath had been an attack on every level of meaning, the dirtying of what had long seemed pure, and the deprivation of every formerly reliable refuge. The physical breathlessness I had experienced for months afterwards was an effect of the panic felt by someone who had run out of places to hide. It occurred to me in stages that a large part of the desperation was cultural. The humane social-democratic culture, with its openness, tolerance and curiosity, that my librarian parents had enjoyed and helped build, was unmistakeably over. Everything I saw from the windows of buses and trains, when walking around town, when reading the news, manifested material ugliness and spiritual indifference. It didn't really help in an immediate way, but at least I understood that I wasn't responsible for my sickness. My individual case, my 'burnout', was caused by the same thing, acting at a personal level, that on different scales dirtied the world for profit, imposed insecure contracts for profit, severed every priceless human relation and marketized human weakness for profit.

Beyond the immediate service they provided as catalysts of memories that could briefly restore me to a lost world, I came to see that on a deeper level the Eardlem objects really did constitute a navigational aid away from hopelessness and towards at least the possibility of some renewed purpose. They were helpful negatively in showing me the futility of trying to live in the past, and also positively, because their very survival seemed to express some potential – perhaps even some desire – to again be part of a living culture. And this final thought gave birth to another: that the objects couldn't achieve this new purposefulness without me. While I hadn't been responsible for what had brought me low, I would have to take responsibility for raising myself up again. And although it only became fully visible in later retrospect, I believe that even at the time, this new thought gave me confidence, for with responsibility comes purpose and pride.

A couple of years before Grandma's death I had bought a double CD of recitals by Paul Robeson, the great African-American singer, actor and activist, whose songs I had heard, off and on, since childhood. One song in particular had caught my attention, not only for its driving rhythm and the customary power of Robeson's delivery but particularly for its lyrics and the story they told. The song, called 'Joshua Fit the Battle of Jericho', is sung as a duet with Robeson's friend and collaborator, the singer and pianist Lawrence Brown. The author of the song is unknown, and many believe that in fact it had no single composer, instead arising out of an oral tradition among enslaved African-Americans in the modern United States, some time in the early 1800s. It's one of those songs that tend to be called 'timeless' – meaning, I think, that that they seem simultaneously to capture and transcend their circumstances, being place- and time-specific yet universal. Straightforwardly an account of the capture by the Israelites of the Canaanite city of Jericho, the song's reference to the breaking of walls also speaks with extraordinary force to the faith and defiance of the enslaved African-Americans. But this level of meaning is enhanced, not diminished, by the recognition that the song also speaks to the whole of humanity, articulating a common desire for rest, sanctuary and home.

The song takes the form of a dialogue: the first speaker asks 'brother pilgrim' where he is bound, and receives this reply:

My name it is poor pilgrim,
To Canaan I am bound.
Travelling through this wilderness
On the disenchanted ground.

I had heard the word disenchantment used before to describe the state to which greed and a lack of care has driven the Earth. It had felt right, but before I listened to this song again I had not really related it to myself. Now it seemed to sum up where I was: I was on disenchanted ground. We all were. The ground was disenchanted because the violent uprooting of human cultures and natural ecosystems, and their supplanting by 'networks' of transactions, long in process, was now rampant and unignorable. But though the adversary seemed anonymous, all-pervasive and abstract, too big and shapeless to be opposed, I retained a shaky faith that this was not the case. The world had become disenchanted because of myriad but theoretically knowable concrete decisions, instances of exploitative action or neglectful inaction, taken by particular groups and individual people in specific places and at specific times. And all the names given to disenchantment – neoliberalism, financialization, deregulated capitalism – were finally just extrusions into history of the selfish aspects of our common human makeup. The workings of disenchantment are known, or at least knowable, and can therefore be reversed.

I realized that I had made some progress over the last few months since the funeral. At first, a combination of the dream-beasts and Ian Hamilton Finlay's lucid axiom had obliged me to see that for years I had been repressing panic about the environmental crisis and the apparent bleeding away of humane civilization. But I was also shown that, perhaps partly because of these things, I had arrived in adulthood without having grown a mature self, a lack which I experienced in the aftermath of Grandma's passing as a great and seemingly sudden disorientation. The beasts and Finlay had laid this lostness bare, and as a reflex I had flailed back to Grandma and Eardlem as the site of my most recent, painful and immediate loss, newly desperate for a fixed point against which to place myself in the present.

But in returning to Eardlem in my imagination I had been confronted by the fact that its loss had also in some way severed me from my own sense of self. I had left much of my innocence there and I could not bring it back. As a stable mooring in the face of all my life's many other changes – changes of house, job, friends – the continuity of my life in Eardlem, over decades, had upheld what I now felt to have been a complacent feeling of self and belonging. Now that security was gone, I slowly came to realize that the loss of my past-self-in-Eardlem would need to be made good if I were to become, as I desperately wished, a source of stability for my own children. Eardlem, as the source – or so I thought – of my deepest lifelong sense of belonging, was still crucial, but there was now a shift of emphasis: *I* was the thing that would have to be 'fixed' if I was to stand a chance of placing everything else. I had willed it the other way round: I had wanted Eardlem to be my fixity. But you can't place yourself in relation to something that isn't, after all, stable, much though you would like it to be. The past of Eardlem is gone, and its present is disenchanted. The very world is disenchanted, and because not enough care was paid to the warnings of Carl Sagan and others, nor to what our own senses were telling us, the very innocence of the past is disenchanted also.

So I had to begin with myself. But where to start? Thrown back on myself, I felt like the proverbial Baron Munchausen, who tried to pull himself out of a swamp by his own hair.

Yet the lesson of the Eardlem objects – the peeler, the fire-screen and their confrères – was that my self is not a helpless, lonely ego, but is shared in its longings and affections, beyond the body's lovely confines, with other people, other beings, other things. There seemed, after all, hope of restoring connection, purpose and community. I had come this far, and was encouraged. But there was plainly much still to do, if I could only work out how. If the severance from Eardlem was in one way a red herring, if the more serious schism was between my former innocent and whole self and my present bleak and riven one, then any hope of further progress would depend on fixing my relationship with myself. But how?

Again at the point of despairing, I thought about the lyrics of that old song 'Joshua Fit the Battle of Jericho'. I opened the laptop and played it, then played it again. Very often, desperate people go in search of themselves too literally and directly. They confront themselves, loud and uncouth, demanding that the soul give an account of itself in plain language, forgetting that the paths to the self are many and obscure. In such a condition, people may overlook the insight that our real selves are often revealed by pseudonyms and that, as in the Greek theatre, truth is best spoken through masks. I listened to the song and smiled. If I wanted to know who I was, then the answer was pretty obvious: I was poor pilgrim. This would be my provisional identity, and it was a good start. In the song, poor pilgrim identifies himself in relation to his destination; the existence of Canaan is what allows him to define himself as a pilgrim in the first place. It was like the witches and the twigs all over again: the key was a relationship, a reciprocity. And then I had a new thought: perhaps belonging isn't a fixed state at all, in the sense of something unchangeable and time-immune, but precisely a relation. Canaan remains abstract and unreal until the pilgrim moves towards it, though perhaps it is sometimes glimpsed as a mirage ahead. But the pilgrim, in turn, becomes more certain of who he is to the degree that Canaan comes to seem increasingly real.

But in that case, if it wasn't Eardlem as such, then what was, is, 'Canaan'? Where is it, and how do you get there? How can a poor pilgrim even embark without some sense of where he is going and what he hopes to find there? And how should he find his way, anyway, across disenchanted ground – a liquid, shifting ground without landmarks? Not only this, but a ground that uproots us all in time as well as in space. For we are stuck, it seems, in the perpetual present of consumer capitalism, in which the past is merely a source of nostalgia or entertainment, and the future is a different combination of the same ingredients in your burger bun. No wonder I had mislaid part of myself while growing up in a society subject to constant upheavals, constant shocks and waves of disenchantment.

I didn't have anything like satisfactory answers to the problem of my fractured identity, and it seemed that if I was to make any progress on my pilgrimage along the cracked road, then to begin with I would have to steer by faith and instinct alone. More than anything it felt obscurely important not to foreclose anything or be satisfied with temporary relief – with 'feeling happier'. After all, it is the very business of the disenchanting forces to make you 'happy' in some trivial and self-indulgent sense. No, happiness was something I would not trust. To the extent that recovery had to begin with myself, it would therefore involve something far beyond some private return to functioning 'wellness'. I had to hold on to the knowledge that the shock to my roots in my childhood and my family also afflicted, albeit almost intangibly, my relationship to sustaining communities of objects and people, to my society and culture, to the natural world, to the Earth and Time itself. I was adrift, but the way back, the way towards 'fixing' myself, in space and time, could not be just individual and personal. The illusion that individuals are separate from each other and the Earth is itself a product of the attitude that is disenchanting us, that is literally killing us. I had to keep in view and rearticulate, over and over, that this is how the profit system replicates itself – by displacing everything and everyone, severing relationships and rendering invisible the very question of how we might reconnect the life of a person with a family, a community, a trade union, a nation, a planet. The free market is a jealous god, intolerant of every relation except that between eight billion lonely, needy individuals and itself. This, perhaps, was the true nature of the dark riddle that had been undermining me for years, but which only the latest local collapse in belonging and identity caused by Grandma's death had forced me to confront.

And it already felt like modest progress to have realized that the riddle could not be opposed in the abstract. After all, the darkness had become visible to me through a specific event, the loss of the family ecosystem of Eardlem as a place that I had known and felt rooted in. I knew that I therefore had to be concrete and go step by step. You can't heal psychic wounds by railing against impersonal forces and abstract nouns – against capitalism and neoliberalism and all the other -isms and -ifications. The path to confronting these things has to be made visible at first by frequent, lonely but determined forays into tangible desolations.

But I stress again that at this time, throughout the summer and into the autumn of 2020, I was only just beginning to intuit these things, and could not feel them cleanly, still less speak them. The dominant feeling was still grief for Grandma and the loss of Eardlem, and the desire to somehow retrieve that place and the lives it had held, including my own. I remained puzzled and frustrated at the mental barriers I hit every time I tried to progress with such retrieval, which suggested a truth that I was extremely unwilling to allow. Could it be, proposed an insistent inner voice, that I was trying to fetch more lost meaning from Eardlem than I had actually ever felt for it? The thought was disconcerting, to say the least. Had I then not loved the place enough? Had I taken it too much for granted? But if these things were true, then why was it the loss of Grandma and Eardlem, in particular, that had broken the dam I had been constructing and unconsciously reinforcing for years against feelings of futility and panic – against disenchanted ground?

Yet gradually that autumn, yielding by minute degrees to these whispered suggestions, I began to accept that there was some truth in them. And I started to think that a breakthrough could only become possible if I shed my guilt and accepted that, although I had unquestionably belonged in my grandparents' house, had known it intimately since I had first toddled into the back garden – Grandma's steady hand helping me over the step – to look at the cows passing down the field, the rest of Eardlem had only ever been mine in a superficial way. Yes, from my late teens and into my thirties I had occasionally returned to visit Grandma and walked, with her or alone, around the village and for perhaps five miles of farmland all around. I knew my way around the lanes, knew which field held the bull, knew the way to the church at Barthomley just across the border into Cheshire, with its effigy of a beautiful lady lying in the cool, pollen-smelling chapel, flying serenely through time on a stone coffin lid.

But as enjoyable, as meaningful, as these visits had been and will always be for me, I had not used these walks as anything but an opportunity for mental rest and to exercise my curiosity. What places I could name along the way I knew not from my own experience but vicariously from Grandma's more intimate knowledge or from the abstractions of maps. I had never been part of the life of the village, had never lived there, was too shy to speak to people, even. If Eardlem felt distant now, I had to admit that I had never looked at it except at a certain distance. No, Eardlem beyond the walls of my grandparents' house had never been mine. And I could see more clearly now that it never could have been. It is possible for a person to be so thoroughly lost in his own life that he cannot articulate what has been lost, much less recover it. I had thought that this was a simple story about my disorientation following the death of my grandmother and the place where she had belonged. But now I was certain that part of my unease arose from not being as dismayed by that as I felt I should have been.

When I had visited Eardlem, one of the walks I took was to a place called Bignall Hill, where at the end of the 'nineties you could still find small numbers of the grey partridge that used to be such a common farmland bird in Staffordshire and all over the British Isles. I would set off from the house with Grandad's binoculars bumping against my chest, following the gloomy cutting of the old colliery rail line before treading my own path of bent grass stems up from the foot of the hill to the Wedgewood Monument at the top. From Bignall Hill it is scarcely more than twenty miles north to a more celebrated piece of high ground – the sandstone scarp of Alderley Edge. Standing among cider cans on the monument's stone plinth, I would train the binoculars on that misty outcrop, which from the age of ten I had known as the home of the writer Alan Garner.

Not the themes only, but even the manner of Garner's writing are inseparable from his choice to return in adulthood, and then spend his entire mature life, in the place where he was raised and where the history of his family is buried deeper than history can tell. Garner has often written and spoken about the fracture in the mind and in one's sense of belonging when for reasons of work, class or education a native son or daughter moves away from the old familial place to be educated in a city which, even though it be close as the crow flies, may as well be in a foreign country for all it has in common with the old family culture in which history and myth blend by long contact into a rich stew.

As a boy Garner's intellect was spotted and had him plucked off Alderley Edge as though by some alien force. He was filtered by the education system to grammar school in Manchester and then to university in Oxford. He was dressed for the life of an academic, but could not settle to it. He felt with intensity the deep rift that his departure into the modern education system had driven between him and his family, who remained on and near Alderley Edge, where Garners had lived for centuries. So he went home, not out of sentiment or nostalgia but for the sake of his mind and his art. He returned and stepped right into the breach that had been made between him and his ancestors. He settled back on Alderley Edge and, as is said of characters at the end of fairy tales, has remained there ever since. His writing, from the 1960s onwards, has been in a very pure way the life's work of inhabiting that breach, acknowledging it but also progressively healing it by writing about it and practising his own form of craftsmanship, different in kind but perhaps close in spirit to the physical craftsmanship of his forebears. In one of the notebooks in which I had sought early manifestations of the dream-beasts, I had come across a quotation from Garner: 'Everywhere is special in some way. It was not imperative that I should be born in Cheshire; but it was imperative that I should know my place. That can only be achieved by inheriting one's childhood landscape and growing in it to maturity. It is a subtle matter of owning and being owned.'

Thinking again about this statement from the study of my Swansea house, towards the end of 2020, I related it to what I had recently come to believe about the reciprocity of people's relationships to material objects. Yes, it is important to know a place, but Garner says that in order for this to happen properly the place also has to know us. In fact it has to know us so well that we are 'owned', or perhaps better say 'possessed' by it, since possession retains the idea that we are taken over or inhabited by something outside, and greater than, our everyday selves. If we do consider returning, like Garner, to the family acre, we may be tempted by the promise that by being fed again at the source of life we will make more of ourselves, although in a sense absolutely opposed to that other type of character who leaves home and travels to the city to 'make something of himself'. Here is a collision of two incompatible archetypes. One cannot go and also stay, stay yet also go. This sounds banal, but it seems to me precisely our fate or condition as modern people to waver in limbo between imagined rootedness and imagined independence. I think we would rather not accept this: we would much prefer to choose a fictitious third option in which we can both be self-inventing yet also belong. It is impossible, and though reason and the will rebel against it, writers and myth-makers know it very well. Indeed, so absolute is this choice between belonging and self-creation that when one is achieved the other ceases to look like a choice. The vale between them is filled with fog, and what once seemed a tangible alternative now appears fantastical, if it is still visible at all.

For the great majority of British people, our relationship to the place where our family is rooted is at least once removed. Like Alan Garner, both of my parents had been educated away from the cultures of their upbringing. I wondered whether, by now, Mum would even claim that she really belonged in Eardlem. At the age of eighteen she had left the village to attend library college in Birmingham, and since then I didn't think she had ever been back to live there, though of course she visited very often.

It's a mark of our family's reticence that I had never really enquired about Mum's childhood. But after rereading what Garner had written, I felt it was time to get close to Eardlem in a different way from that made possible by my mental flights in the company of the vegetable peeler. Mum had been born there, grown up there, throughout her childhood had really belonged there. She had, in Garner's words, 'grow[n] in it to maturity'. I wanted to know what that had been like. She is, after all, the last living link to Eardlem, the last member of our close family to have really known it. But beyond my ordinary, personal interest in finding out about Mum's early life, partly under Garner's influence I now also had something else in mind. Eardlem may never have been my home, but it was the closest thing I had to a native place. If I could begin to understand what it used to be like, and how the postwar 'great acceleration' of capital deregulation had changed it, then this could be a way of plotting my pilgrimage across disenchanted ground and of using, rather than passively suffering, the cracks that, as I newly understood them, connect individual, private suffering to the land of the dead that lies just over our common horizon.

6

From my childhood home in Birmingham my mum called Grandma every Sunday on the foursquare, puce-coloured Bakelite phone that squatted on our hall table, joined to the wall and the international telecommunications system by an irresistibly twangable spiral cord. After Grandma died the habit passed down wordlessly, and now it is Mum and I who speak almost every Sunday. I usually video call her from the kitchen so that the children can say hello, or later at night from the study at the top of the house, where as I listen to her I watch the lighthouse fling its beam around the bay. One Sunday just before Christmas I ask whether I can come up and stay. I'm working on a book about Eardlem. Would she mind if I visited and asked a few questions? I can only get so far with my own memories, and I want to know more about her childhood in Eardlem, and how she feels about the place now.

In late January I travel up by bus. Mum still lives in Birmingham, in a first-floor flat at the edge of a housing estate behind a McDonald's to the north of the city. From the bus station in Digbeth I walk to New Street and board a local train that's X-rayed by low winter light. It shines right through the carriage and out the other side, rippling the shadows of the passengers' heads across metal fences and heaps of bricks waiting to be turned into something new.

Now Mum has taken away our pasta bowls, and while I clear the table she shakes the cloth out of the window for the birds to find the crumbs. Afterwards she takes down her box files so we can go digging together in the past. I've said that our family are not talkers, and this is no small occasion. I have a tape recorder running – an ancient dusky blue thing the size of a house cat, salvaged from a skip outside a university language school – so I won't later have to rely on my poor memory for what she says as we go slowly through the photographs. Mum wants to know what I'm looking for, exactly, and what I want to know. I say that I honestly can't tell her, that I'm just trying to find my way through things, to look for clues and wait for something to come up, if it ever does. I stop short of telling her about Canaan, but that's the gist. And it's quite true: even after all my recent thinking, my motives are still complicated and obscure even to myself, but fundamentally I think I am trying to root myself, albeit at one remove, in stories that will bind me closer to my family and its history in Eardlem.

Mum sighs and with her fingertips draws a photograph from one of the polypockets in the box file. Beyond the window the winter light is weaker now, thin and pale. When wind shakes the tall willow outside, the light is shadow-patterned by its long leaves. The light laps over the photograph in rapid, barely perceptible licks that mimic the tongue-shapes of the leaves. As we bend together over the photograph there is a near silence in which the thirty-year-old tape machine chunters and purls, the restaurant's extractor fan drones, and a robin's hesitant song soaks note by note through the bricks. It is the winter song, equal parts hope and resignation. Together we look at the photo, which shows me, swaddled and white like a grub, on Grandma's lap, squinting up into the sun behind which my dad will certainly have been pulling faces to hold my attention. This is the first photograph that shows me in Eardlem. We flip through several

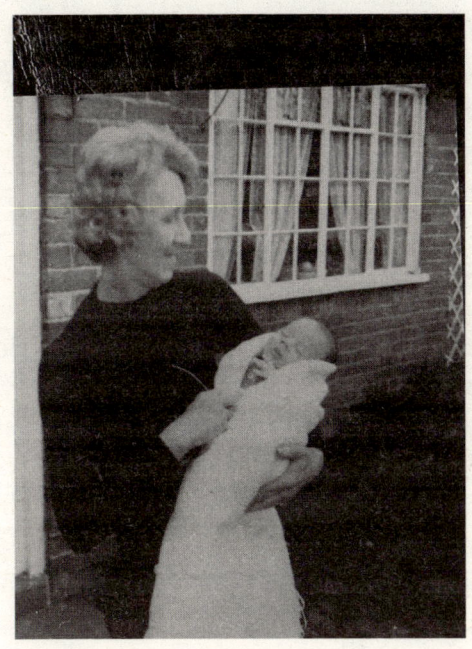

more, passing quickly over some, lingering on others, and then after a while the talk starts to flow naturally, me asking questions prompted by the photos, and Mum reaching back into the past.

I ask about her early memories and she tells me about her first day at infants' school. They must have had an indoor see-saw because mum remembers being stranded in the air when a heavier child sat on the other end. 'I was a skinny little thing'.

'Was school strict?'

'I can't remember. No, not really. We did have elocution lessons. [She puts on her Eliza Doolittle voice] *They tried to get me to talk proper*. I had to stand on a chair once and recite a poem. "Something, something, Ermintrude Annie / Went to the country to visit her grannie / Learned to make butter, learned to make cheese / Learned to make jam and take honey from bees . . ." That's all I can remember.'

We go on talking about school. Her secondary school was a grammar, and she was the first of her family ever to attend such a place. Was she aware of class difference? She says yes, she first noticed it there. None of her friends' families in Eardlem had cars, but most girls at the grammar would get picked up by their parents. She was conscious of her dad being a bus driver.

I just about remember Grandad driving the buses, and especially a visit we must have made one day to the depot. We would have gone there in his jade-green Lada with the leather seats that became so hot in summer that you had to sit on your own hands to stop your thighs burning. I've never cared about vehicles, but I was fascinated by that trip to the depot. It was long, dim-lit and diesel-reeking, the buses poised on jacks like big oily men doing chaturanga. A photo on my study wall shows Grandad in his driver's uniform. He's handsome, Brylcreemed, wears a tie. Come to think of it, he almost always wore a shirt and tie, except, Mum is saying, when he drove pensioners to Weymouth by charabanc for their annual outing, when he'd change into a white coat and hat. But that was just as a novelty. I smile as she tells about a time they offered him a promotion to inspector, but he declined in part because he wouldn't wear the cap that came with the office. He was a principled egalitarian and didn't want to wear anything that would set him above his colleagues. He didn't want anyone to feel inferior to him, and he didn't respect rank for its own sake. It was the same during the war, Mum is saying, when he was forever being given kitchen chores for refusing to kowtow to the officers. Grandad was well-liked by his colleagues, and on his retirement he was given the watch that I am wearing now. On the back is an inscription:

Presented to John Bernard Williams by the Potteries Motor Traction Co. Ltd., in appreciation of 25 years loyal service. 1979.

After Grandad died, the bus company was privatized, and not long afterwards services from Eardlem to the local towns were decimated, and many lines rerouted. I remember Grandma talking about this in a fury on one of the trips I made to see her when I was in my twenties: she was angry and, I think, *ashamed* on behalf of an 'elderly' neighbour – Grandma herself was in

her eighties at the time – who now couldn't go into Hanley to do her shopping. 'If it leaves one person behind, then it's not a service, is it!'

Mum says that in the 1960s Grandad would sometimes take her to the pictures in Hanley. They saw *The Parent Trap* and *In Search of the Castaways*, so perhaps Grandad had a thing about Hayley Mills. Meanwhile at home the wireless still mainly played 'Kalamazoo' and 'Like a Golden Dream', but 'Jailhouse Rock' and 'Tutti Frutti' were already on Radio Luxembourg, and two years later, in 1964, *Top of the Pops* would bring the new youth culture into the living room through their rented television. And for her eighteenth birthday Grandma and Grandad bought Mum a transistor radio. Hers was the first generation in which teenagers could sequester themselves away with portable music – the technology causing new physical divisions in domestic space.

Mum talks and I listen, while the willow-leaf shadows rise slowly from the settee and begin to flutter on the far wall. Of course, much of the conversation centres on Grandma, and towards the end of our talk Mum surprises me by looking up from the box file and saying 'Sometimes I feel like I'm turning into her'. I ask her what she means, and Mum says that she was coming up the stairs to her flat the other day and saw herself as though from the outside, in exactly Grandma's manner and posture.

At the bottom of one box file is a slim red notebook. This is the Red Book of family lore, a seven-page account, typed by Grandma towards the end of her life, of memories of her childhood. Mum had already photographed its contents and forwarded them to me by email, but it is a different thing to have it open on my knees. The book begins with a memory from 1923 or 1924:

The earliest recollections of my life must have been when I was not more than three years old. I can clearly see, placed beneath the kitchen window, a bassinette in which lay my baby brother Fred, who was born twenty months after myself. My mother, Harriet, had long black hair which, for every day, she wore in plaits round her ears like headphones. On that occasion she was seated on a kitchen chair with her hair released from its many pins and cascading down her back. Behind her, on another chair, I stood brushing her tresses.

We read more from the Red Book, and intersperse it with other, unwritten stories that we both remember Grandma telling about her life in the 1920s and 1930s. So much knowledge has disappeared, but we must be grateful for what we have. It occurs to me then, perhaps for the first time, that the knowledge is not just in us but *is* us. Grandma is alive in mum's body as she sees herself uncannily on the stairs. I think back to the children's changing faces in their annual school photographs, in which the features of myself and their mother, uncles and aunts, four grandparents and who knows how many past generations are recorded, some fleetingly and others as a constant likeness.

It is nearly time for me to return to Wales, but as I press 'stop' on the recorder and pack my rucksack, I have a sudden desire to see the house where I grew up. It is only two miles away from Mum's flat, but I haven't been there for nearly twenty years. Looking at all those old childhood photographs must have sown the desire to see it again. Mum, forever cautious about time, is not sure that we can do it, but I cajole her, saying I only want to look at the place for five minutes. It's not as if we're going to knock on the door or anything.

It is a haunted thing to return to one's childhood home. I could feel it already as Mum turned off the main road and we climbed the cul-de-sac.

Of my earliest years I remember only warmth and light. After several refusals Mum and Dad had found a bank willing to advance them a mortgage and bought for £6,000 a semi-detached, brick house in the suburb of Kingstanding. In doing so, as far as we know, they were the first generation of either family to own their own home. Both my parents worked in libraries. Mum had a job at an industrial library in Wolverhampton, now closed but still in community use as a gurdwara. Sometimes she went up there on the train, and sometimes she drove in the purple mini with a white stripe that had set them back £50. Dad managed the branch library at Aston and later, around the time of my birth, successfully applied for money to found a new library in an untenanted flat in the poor inner-city district of Newtown, with the express intention of breaking down barriers to culture among the urban working class, many of them recently arrived migrants from South Asia and the Caribbean. It's hardly conceivable now, but in the mid 1970s there was both the imagination and the funding to make such initiatives work. It was very important to Dad that libraries should also be places of adult literacy. That was a civilized time which wasn't to be maintained.

I was born, and kept Mum in hospital for a week. When we came home, Dad was for a while displaced from the bed and slept instead on a fake-leather armchair which, like all of the other furniture in the house, had been bought on hire purchase. This was just as a cool spring gave way definitively to a long, hot summer, and when we came home I was to spend much of my time outside in a carrycot. When it was too hot I must have been laid indoors in a crib from where I watched dust motes floating in the sunbeams. When I was upset, Mum, twenty-six years old, would lift me up and sing,

> Go to sleep my baby
> Close your pretty eyes
> When you wake, you'll be so happy
> We shall have such fun
> So, go to sleep my baby
> Go to sleep my son.

The song was her own composition but she repeated it so often that many years afterwards, when she was on stage acting the part of Linda Loman in *Death of a Salesman* and the script required her to hum a melody, this lullaby was what came to her first.

I believe that enchantment is natural to us. Perhaps ordinarily the mother's body is the first enchanted ground, but it expands quickly to another parent or carer, to a cot and bedding, a room, siblings, grandparents, the house, the garden. Object by object, the world is annexed to enchantment, and the infant receives these objects, whether human or not, as persons. Formal religion may be taught later, but animism is easy and fundamental. It is not true that a newborn is only a hungry little ego. There is always something else, beside and beyond it, something unbiddable, like a grace. Unpredictably, the nursery will be illuminated by light and warmth. The colours of the wallpaper, the sleep-suit, the quilt, become suddenly intense; objects one thought one knew are transfigured and shadow-twinned; the light finds new possibilities in them. Surfaces glow, the very air is filled with exuberant dust that the infant's fist reaches for in delight but cannot grasp or exhaust. The light is not a given, so it is naturally and rightly treated as a gift. And the light does not simply work physically on objects, but spiritually, on a part of the growing person that is inner but not ego. The light, and the silence it brings with it, stirs a longing in the child for something that it cannot wish to own. It is ours but can never be beckoned down, still less possessed. What can it be?

I believe that I was aware of this mysterious extra from early on. I did nothing to cultivate it, and for long periods I was presumably oblivious of it, being occupied by other, more tangible sorts of nourishment: toys, increasingly large mounds of pasta, the overwhelming physical thrill of a good tickle. But every child has, or should have, abstracted moments that seem to belong to a different branch of growth. These are the minutes when, staring out of the window at the rain falling on the garden, bored into inertia, some sort of alchemy starts up and the boredom shades imperceptibly to absorption. The mind falls quiet, feels empty. And with nothing else to distract it, it starts to see what it had not seen before: how the soil darkens beneath the mild rain, how the blackbird stops to listen for worms beneath the lawn, how the trees shiver ecstatically in the wind one cannot hear. The child's chin is on the windowsill; he must be uncomfortable in that position, kneeling on the carpet for so long, but his body seems relaxed. You have come into the room to ask him to do something but now you too are caught by the silence of the room, and something else that the silence is kin to. Things have changed. It's as if instead of the window looking out onto the garden, the garden has crept closer and has pressed its huge green face to the glass. It sees the room. It sees the boy. And the boy is on the border, as on the threshold between waking and sleeping. You pause at the entrance of the room and, looking at him again, your mouth closes on the instruction you had prepared. You exit the room backwards, and close the door in silence.

As I grew, I came to understand these moments at the turnstile of the self as a vital source of food. And since they were in every case provoked by a feeling of the presence of the natural world, I began to desire time alone 'in nature'. Not that the feeling could ever be summoned, no more in boyhood than when I had lain in the cot. But a delight in the independent life of birds and animals, of the mutual affection of wind and water and sun, fed into the part of me that differed from the part which enjoyed football and computer games.

The only other activity that could approximate this feeling was reading: the abandonment or loosening of the everyday self was similar. But its purest form was met in encounters with wild creatures. Some of these were very local. Outside the front door, just beside the garden path, was our vulcanized rubber waste bin, with a dented lid where rainwater collected. The bin was in the shade of a laurel bush, and behind the laurel was a cherry tree whose extending branches added to the grotto-like feel of the area around the bin. Some combination of the shade, the water and the stillness of the air in this corner of the garden attracted gnats, and at almost any time of year a column of these almost transparent insects would oscillate there. Sometimes I would try to disrupt the cloud, swishing through it with a stick or my arm. Not every impulse we are born with is benign, and sometimes I viciously desired to provoke a reaction from what was so obviously content without me. But in a different mood I would simply keep still and watch the gnats. Through watching I came to admire them, and over time this admiration turned into something like love. I find it hard to say whether I most loved the gnats themselves or the mere fact that they were there. But yes, I surely loved a great deal about them. I loved the shapes they made in the air, I loved their silent 'g'. I loved the courtliness of their interactions and the way they were sometimes lit by a bar of sunlight tinted green-maroon by the cherry tree while they danced their silent and most ancient mazurkas.

We pull up in front of the house, and the first shock is that the tall semicircle of sentinel leylandiis are no longer there. Instead there is a driveway for two cars and a neat little lawn. That's the whole trouble with the past: it is not there.

7

The phone with which Mum and Grandma kept in touch crouched on a table at the foot of the staircase. At the top of the stairs was the landing with a hatch in its ceiling, which was the entrance to the loft. And though the loft had in no way been made safe, at intervals throughout the 1980s my father would take us up there for a slide show. We ascended by a concertinaed wooden ladder whose metal hinges had a taste for human flesh. The ladder slept within the loft itself, so Dad first had to retrieve it. A kitchen chair was waddled upstairs, and after he had satisfied himself that it sat stably Dad climbed on to it and then stretched up to dislodge, by blows of the palm, the truculent whitewashed trap-door. It always took a few smacks, but finally the hatch was sent rattling away into the invisible interior of the loft, to be replaced in the ceiling by a black square into which Dad would reach for the dangling toggle of the light switch and then for the near edge of the ladder, all of this watched impatiently from the landing by the uptilted faces of my sister and me.

The loft space wasn't large, and the part laid over with ply-board was smaller still, so that sitting on it felt precarious and exciting, like being on a rowing boat in the dark. Once we'd been up there for a few minutes, we could appreciate that the darkness wasn't total. Light seeped in everywhere through fissures in the brickwork, randomly spotlighting old suitcases as though they contained not our ordinary outgrown clothes but the aureoled shinbones of saints. The area around the chimney stack was particularly light-riddled, and in 1985 it illuminated for the first time the bulging paper citadel of an enormous wasps' nest and the sinister drifting apostrophes of the insects themselves as they processed to and fro through the largest crack in the brickwork. The extraordinary nest was left unmolested that year, and the slide show was postponed. But the following spring an exterminator was summoned and the nest and its residents were destroyed by some yellow and evil-smelling powder that settled everywhere and coated our hands for years afterwards like the fingerprint powder applied at a crime scene.

Dad climbed the final rungs and the black square swallowed him, his paddling ankles last to be ingested. After a few seconds his framed head would reappear, youthful, bearded and smiling, to give my sister and me permission to join him, Mum following behind in case either of us should miss a rung. Once we'd all made it, we were settled, cross-legged, sweaty and itching from the wasp poison, on the plywood before a mobile projector screen mounted on a metal stand borrowed from Birmingham Library Services. While Dad fussed with the slide boxes behind us, the screen registered his movements in weird looping shadows, which, just as the children of Lascaux would have done, we augmented with improvised finger-shadows of fauna real and imagined. Even prior to the gassing of the wasps, the hot, stale air was unpleasant to breathe, seeming at least two-thirds dust, and we fidgeted uncontrollably until at last Dad hushed us and announced that the slide show was to begin. Remember this was before the internet, and our minds were not yet sick with images. So you may imagine our excitement as we stared in expectant silence at that white canvas screen. There is a false start as the first side fails to load. A juddering slapstick twang, muffled by brickwork, means the woodpigeon has just launched off the TV aerial.

From his position beside the slide tray, with the aid of a torch, Dad can read what's written on the sticky labels on the back of each slide. His voice comes out of the darkness. 'April 19, 1976. The day Steven should have been born.' At last, an unfocused image blazes in from the side of the screen, slops around violently like sunshine in a bucket, and then after a last wild wobble, settles. With perfect clarity we are shown Mum, upside down in a floral maternity dress, dangling from the top of the picture like a serene and colossal bat. 'Damn!' shouts Dad. My sister and I begin to hoot. Mum maintains a silence that could either be dignified or sarcastic. There's much huffing from the darkness behind us as Dad fumbles to reinsert the slide with the misplaced label. Then we start again.

Mum is standing stiffly upright, the better to show the enormous bulge under her frock. She is smiling through her tiredness and looks very beautiful, her mouth slightly open as though she were arrested in the act of saying something to Dad behind the camera. Either the photo is slightly overexposed or it was one of those days of bright high cloud on which colours anyway seem bleached. The white sky behind her glares brightly enough to make shadows of the bloom-bearing branches of the apple tree that overhung the fence to next door's garden. Mum's right hand is clenched, though if she is anxious or in discomfort her face doesn't show it. She looks completely at home with the things around her, with the white light of April 1976, on the cusp of that famously long, hot summer that was assumed to be a once-in-a-century freak.

Ordinarily, I doubt whether children think of themselves as belonging to a generation. There are simply other children around you to be idolized, tolerated or avoided, your parents,

who are old but will never get older, and your grandparents, who
are so old that it is not worth thinking about. All adults, really,
are simply there, like trees and clouds. As a child you have no
critical distance from anything and no other experiences against
which to draw comparisons, so you accept everything around
you as a fact. It wasn't until I was in my thirties, had children of
my own and saw for the first time undeniable evidence of my parents ageing, that I began to wonder what continuities or ruptures
there had been between my childhood and the childhoods of the
generations on either side. And it was only in the aftermath of
Grandma's death, in trying to work through my own confusion
about belonging so that I could 'fix' myself against a background
of disenchantment, that I began to search for the *essence* of my
childhood – one lived in the suburbs of an English city at the end
of the 1970s and the early 1980s.

One way to reach towards the essence of a time is to accumu-
late so much material detail that gradually a shape and texture
become perceptible through it, as magnetic force becomes visible under a shower of iron filings. Since our young minds must
make sense of so much that seems indiscriminate, the accumu-
lated facts must also be of different scales. As a six-year-old
I was launching a two-inch-long Pontiac Firebird (note the
American make) repeatedly off the arm of the settee. Behind
me the Falklands War, shrunk to a 12-inch screen, was being
fought at a twelve-hour lag. The ice-cream van, chiming 'Girls
and boys come out to play' would turn up the cul-de-sac, and
I'd rush outside in my socks, invariably pulping a fallen cherry
or two whose cool damp stain soaked through to my feet. It
was summer, and though of course I didn't know it then, the
taste of the vanilla ice cream with raspberry sauce would be
associated for ever after with the smell of the jasmine in flower

next door. Or at about the same age, but in winter, I see myself crouched in the back garden, using Mum's pilfered cochineal to flood with colour the ice palaces I'd compacted from the snow. Small birds flitted to the feeder in the bare trees above the lollipop crosses of the hamster graveyard, while dislodged gobbets of suet made little meltwater craters on the surface of the ice; in the kitchen the braised steak was bubbling and the beef smog was salivating at the windows. On the radio all the politicians – who, irrespective of party allegiance, you could still refer to without wincing as 'statesmen' – began with 'H' and the presenter conjugated Hurd, Hume, Healey, Haughey and Howe, all to a background soundtrack of 'Nellie the Elephant', filtering through from the living room where my sister sat clapping on her thighs with her hands.

I think that all of this, every perception and experience, must enter a child for ever. But even if it were possible to reconstruct each impression, would the sum of these things constitute the child's self, or is there something else there to begin with? An inner force that makes of the common experiences of a generation something irreducible and unique, a shared interior life that can be partially reconstructed in memory? In the angle at which the sun's light strikes the earth, in the tilt of the stars, in the pitch of the wind and the look of the woods, in the flickering colours under the cherry tree and in the inks of old motoring manuals, in the bitter taste of the leylandii pods mixed in potions and the smell of the spice rack you once experimentally set alight, in the smell of your father's skin and your newborn sister's first furze of hair, through the hiss of the turntable and the clatter of the slide projector, in the old soul peering from a new body like an owl from its nest-hole, in the hot shame of punishment and the bliss of mote-filled boredom and the Sunday-morning sumo on *Trans*

World Sport. These times and combinations can ever reoccur, but they remain real for as long as we carry them inside us.

From behind us comes a startling and quite unnecessarily prolonged sneeze, and Mum, my sister and I all retract our heads. 'Excuse me!' Dad has been groping in the dusty projector bag for the clicker, and returned in triumph. The slides will hopefully change a little quicker for it.

In the slide I must be around four years old. I am in Sutton Park, a vast, improbable survivor of a ninth-century hunting forest, where we often came and where my soul was early fed. The photo was taken by Dad, who was into photography at that time and enjoyed trying out different filters and exposures, though in truth the light of the park is already pre-stained by the sepia of longing. Whether it is in dim

memory or later imagination I see Dad very clearly, hunkered in the
bracken with his lens raised and a smile on his face as he watches the
utter transfixion of his son by the browns of the wood, the branches,
the light and shadow, the smell of overripe sap released by my small
bootfall. I am wearing a brown duffle-coat with veined tawny toggles.
I have, it must be admitted, a horrendous 'bowl-head' fringe. My head
is still too large for my body. I do not know and I do not care. My face
is serious but rapt. I am what I appear to be: a young ape in paradise.

We came to the park as often as we could, to walk its root-riddled
paths of pale clay and whitish pebbles that flowed between dark
trees. Near-permanent rain would turn these tracks into streams
that fed the many polished black lakes. When geese appeared,
clamouring, above the tree line, we would watch the lake surface scored silver by their landing. In seconds the water would
close again, sealed no less tightly than by the thick ice of those
departed winters when we took turns to fling stones across the
singing surface, thrilled into silence by the hollow fluting tones
thrown back by the vast frozen eardrum of the lake, the nerves in
our necks tingling. There was one spot we came to often. A wet
plain of grass and gorse with a knoll in the centre crowned with
trees. I called it the fairy ring, but its magic was merely an especially obvious outgrowth of an otherworldliness that suffused the
atmosphere of the entire park. Did I feel at home in the park, then
or at any time subsequently when as a young adult I returned to
it half-consciously for succour? It's impossible for a human being
to feel at home in such a place, but this unhomeliness is the very
stuff of its gift. As surely as those stones whistling over the skin
of ice sounded the depth of the lake, so to walk the park's surface
is to open yourself to soundings from below, from within, from
parts of yourself whose presence you could never speak of nor

dare question. This is why I revere the park, which remains the source of my lifelong recognition that only when alone in wood, mountain, or marsh do I ever come close to finding something I think of as myself.

Taken at sunset in the back garden at Eardlem. Two horses are staring at the photographer. If the sun were any higher, they would be in silhouette. If it were any lower, they would be barely distinguishable from the field. As it is, the light is just enough to daub a line of pastel brown along their backs. It must be summer, because the hedge behind is tall. Clearly visible are the holes where the cattle have chomped and trampled their way through. Behind the hedge are the two other fields before the row of houses along Nantwich Road. Behind them is the ridge called Kent Hills, with the reservoir building and dark clouds of trees including a single poplar towering up into the clouds of bright, orange-lit cream, like the orange-flavoured fondants we bit into at Christmas. Nantwich Road was formerly called Quarry Road, after the sand and gravel quarries dug into the hill. A photograph from the 1930s shows the road empty of houses but lined with lofty, billowing elms.

New Year's Day, 1984. From left to right, Uncle Jack, Grandad, Grandma and Mum in the back garden at Eardlem, their backs against the fence. There were no flower beds then, no raspberry plants or holly. There's just the wire fence separating the grass of the field from the greener grass of the garden. This isn't a posed photo, and nobody is ready. Jack and Grandad, both wearing shirts and ties, look impatient, Grandad positively cross. Grandma has a blue dress on and some misadjusted jewels thrown around her neck. She is looking at Mum's shoes and, to judge from Mum's face, is making a critical comment about them. Mum's hair is a blondish perm like a judge's wig. Nobody is smiling at all. Yes, everyone looks thoroughly irritated, though not with Dad, who's presumably taking the picture. Grandad and Jack's eyes are looking instead towards the back door, where presumably my sister and I are hesitating, reluctant to join this cranky outfit.

It's the same date as the previous photo, but this is a shot of Grandad alone, seated in his favourite chair in the back room. He has on a thin, lichen-coloured jumper over a stiff white shirt buttoned all the way up and further fixed with a knotted tie. It's just six months until his death, but though he looks old he doesn't seem unwell. He's grimacing humorously while he tugs at his ear with his left hand. His shadow falls on the white wall beside him. Behind the chair is the sideboard, bearing a Wedgewood vase, three paperweights, a pottery figurine of a wagtail and a portrait of me in my primary school uniform.

Labelled '1982?'. Again the back garden at Eardlem. Grandad, my sister and I are in the shot. Grandad is leaning over the fence to stroke the head of a curious cow. My sister is facing the cow, standing close to it with the fence between them. I'm sheltering behind Grandad, visibly nervous. Grandad is smiling and his whole bearing shows affection for the animal. The cow, however, has swivelled its alien eye and is staring straight at the camera.

A car horn sounds behind us and in the mirrors we see someone politely gesturing for us to move. We are blocking the drive. Wrong place. Wrong time.

On the drive back to New Street Mum asks if that's it or whether I'll need to visit again with more questions. I say I'll phone her if I think of anything. She drops me off and I wave until the car disappears.

Then I board my train for Wales.

I'd been in Birmingham for just twenty-four hours, but it had felt like years. Back in Swansea, I reflected that in a sense it really had been. In Mum's living room and recollections, in the word-images of Grandma's Red Book of memories, and in looking from the outside at my own childhood in the house where I had grown up, chamber after chamber had opened up inside me. How much of the past we carry with us always! Like Russian dolls Grandma is in Mum, just as Mum is in me. And since a person is largely an outcome of his or her experiences, somewhere all that has passed is within us too, forever changing us just as, in our neediness and imperfect memories, we are always changing it also.

But clock time has a habit of reasserting itself. The next few days are busy with school assemblies, seminars and proofreading, and it's not until a week later that I find time to sit in the study to play back the interview with Mum. A wind off the bay is wheedling in between the window and the frame; I have Aunty May's cobbled rose garden on my knees and a mug of tea balanced on the bookshelf. Beyond the window I absently notice a pair of magpies fussing around last year's nest. The winter gales have reduced and dishevelled it until it resembles nothing but a small and ragged ball of grey yarn. I press 'rewind', then 'play' and discover that for some reason the first half of the conversation has not been recorded. For a minute I fear I've lost the lot, but then there's a clunking sound and our voices swim up indistinctly out of the hiss, as though the interview had been conducted behind a waterfall. I listen and make notes. When I come to Mum's mention of the poem she learned at school, I press 'pause' and open the laptop to look it up:

Amy Elizabeth Ermyntrude Annie
Went to the country to visit her Grannie;

Learnt to churn butter and learnt to make cheese,
Learnt to milk cows and take honey from bees;

Learnt to spice roseleaves and learnt to cure ham,
Learnt to make cider and black-currant jam.

When she came home she could not settle down,
Said there was nothing to do in the town.

Nothing to do there and nothing to see:
Life was all shopping and afternoon tea!

Amy Elizabeth Ermyntrude Annie
Ran away back to the country and Grannie!

The website had a bit of background about its author, Queenie Scott-Hopper, who died in 1924: 'Her poems and stories seem to have remained popular long after her death and she has appeared in anthologies alongside much more famous poets. She regularly featured in collections compiled for use in schools right up until the early sixties when tastes changed dramatically.'

How much is glossed by that casual statement about changing tastes! Several times, listening to Mum, the thought came to me that if I hadn't known she was describing the 1960s, I might have thought it was a century earlier. But it seems to me that the poem, at least, isn't anything like as frivolous as it's bouncing rhythms and naive rhymes make it appear. How much of an ache seems hidden just beneath – an ache for 'the country and Grannie'.

8

In the wake of the visit to Mum, and later when listening repeatedly to the parts of our conversation captured by the tape machine, it became easier to picture what life in Eardlem used to be like. I was struck by what a self-sufficient community it had been – community not in the tokenistic sense, full of political innuendo, in which that word now tends to be used, but community as a real ecosystem of institutions in which the profit motive had not yet devoured mutualism and tradition. I found it difficult to accept that this was a postwar society, so unrelatable did it seem to my own experience as a child adrift in the suburbs. The fact that community institutions such as Sunday School, the Wakes Week holiday and parade, whist drives in the Band Hall (where Mum had once won a mug with a sheepdog on it), the theatre and community centre had survived the ruptures of war made their sudden disappearance between my parents' generation and my own much starker and more sobering. Grandma and Grandad, also, had spoken of the Wakes and of chapel parades through the village, and it struck me that there had been much more continuity between my grandparents' and parents' generations than between my parents' and my own. With this realization came the understanding that the true cataclysm, the true agent of disenchantment, had not been war but the Great Acceleration of capital accumulation that had sped up immeasurably following the deregulations of the early 1980s, alongside the development of new and alienating technologies. This Great Acceleration, of course, was the name of a concept I had found out about in books, but listening to Mum's account of her childhood made it personal and real.

In the Red Book, Grandma recalls as an extraordinary occasion her first ride in a motor car, on the way to a family wedding in the winter of 1926. By the time my mother was born, cars were everywhere, and the map of the British Isles was newly painted with yellow, red and blue lines – the transport network that in linking together for the purposes of buying and selling places that had existed since Domesday and before also severed them from one another and alienated them from their own histories and the institutions that preserved their special character. A different outcome of the new transport network and an archipelago 'open for business' was that it brought the countryside closer to the children and grandchildren of people who had grown up in it but who had themselves been raised in or near to cities. In a way, perhaps, this is when 'the countryside' was invented, for the new exhortation to business also assumed a redefinition of unpaved land as a potential site for something called 'leisure'.

This is why, for my sister and me, as for Amy Elizabeth Ermyntrude Annie, our grandmother was among other things a synecdoche of the country. I could see now that Eardlem had always unspokenly represented our own idea of that enigmatic English obsession, 'the countryside'. My sister and I were hardly raised in the ghetto: our part of suburban Birmingham was relatively green. Nevertheless, by travelling to Eardlem we exchanged exhaust fumes for the smells of grass and manure, a view of cars for a view of cows, and a fenced prospect of a few metres for a vista over fields to hills that seemed to us the gateway to 'nature', in which all the brightly coloured and sweet-voiced birds of Grandad's field guide dwelt and replaced themselves as they always had and assuredly always would. Now that I could no longer return to that house in Eardlem, I felt the loss of this connection to the land even as I feared what I knew to be true: that the natural ecosystems of my grandparents' and parents' Eardlem had fared no better under capitalist technologies and the mindsets that motivated them than had the cultural ecosystems of village life that Mum was of the last generation to remember.

Yes, I knew, really, that what now passes for the country-side around Eardlem is more green desert than ecosystem. I had known it for a long time, but its new, full, realization was just the latest part of the awakening enabled by the dream-beasts and Ian Hamilton Finlay's exacting maxim. But if I was not to fall into a rather sterile and reactionary nostalgia, I also had to admit complexity. Eardlem had not been a truly rural economy for hundreds of years; the real fixed identity of its life, from the eighteenth through to the mid-twentieth century, had been the coal mines that had fostered communal identity even as they had despoiled the earth, locally and globally. Nevertheless, and trying to avoid simplistic binaries, it was also true that before the coming of industrial agriculture and the supermarkets, much more of the food that sustained the people of Eardlem had come from the land around the village, and that the land had also been richer, almost unimaginably so, in flowers, insects, birds and other animals.

For me, on my occasional visits back to Eardlem throughout the late 1990s and the first twenty years of the present century, circumstance dictated that my bond with the village would have little to do with the landscape. Because of the M6 and other main roads, nowhere you could walk to felt really wild. Again, if any-thing, the distinctive history of the area was preserved more in the towns, with their remnant bottle ovens and forests of buddleia spurting from the necks of old pot banks, than in what might with reservations be referred to as countryside. The character of the land had been too drastically altered by the removal of hedgerows and the imposition of an intensive cattle monoculture. It had been shown too little care, force-fed too many chemicals. Only here and there can you see a big field oak that whether for practical or emotional reasons was spared destruction, or feel a sudden sense of antiquity from some permanently shadowed field hollow that may have been a drinking place for cattle for a thousand years.

But I was fed on a townie's idea of the countryside, and for thirty unthinking years this was enough for me. I loved the stink of silage, which was for me the cleanest smell in the world. Besides, I knew where to find the very few remaining patches of unspoiled land, like Bignall Hill and Town Fields, where in my childhood yellowhammers still sang, though they're long gone now. In those early years of visiting Eardlem, though, when my sister and I were still young, my idea of the countryside was represented by that view from Grandma's back window – those few poor fields fringed by houses, and the green slope beyond up to the reservoir.

Aunty May, my grandad's sister, lived ninety years in Eardlem. We'd visit her most times we went up. She was a kind, funny woman of the 'indomitable' class, sensibly afraid of cows and thunderstorms but little else. It was she who had taken Mum to the Band Hall whist drives in the early 1960s, and Mum remembered with great affection her visits to the house May shared with Uncle Ted, a retired fireman and ardent leftwinger who read the *Tribune*, was constantly tinkering with cars and went rabbiting with ferrets. Forty years later, for my sister and me visits to Aunty May were easier than those to other relatives, and though our lank-haired indie-kid teenage selves sat awkwardly on her sofa, we liked May's unaffected kindness and bluntness. She also told good stories, and one I remember particularly. It was a spring day long ago, she said, just before her birthday. She was playing out in the lanes with her friends, her parents nearby, and all around the corncrakes were making their usual racket in the fields. The sound was so familiar as to go almost unheard, so when the birds suddenly stopped as one the effect was startling, even eerie. When they started up again a few minutes later the incident was forgotten until, upon returning home, the adults learned from the wireless that the *Titanic* had disappeared in the North Atlantic. Then someone remembered the crakes and, reckoning back, it was determined that the birds had fallen silent at exactly the moment the liner had sunk into the icy sea.

My memory is usually poor, so to begin with I was puzzled why this story surfaced in my mind, soon after my trip to Birmingham, after many years' burial. My recall of historical dates is even worse, but when it occurred to me to fact-check the *Titanic* disaster my confusion grew. Aunty May can't have remembered the *Titanic* sinking, because she hadn't been born. Yet she had told the story as her own, and in such detail that I'd almost been able to smell the spring hedges and hear the crakes myself. What was going on, and why did this story have such a hold on me? I now feel sure that what May told us that day in Eardlem *was* absolutely true, but in a deeply non-literal way. The north Staffordshire fields, in common with the whole British countryside, had indeed once creaked with rasping corncrakes. My mother never heard one, though, for by the 1960s they had vanished. More precisely, modern agricultural practices had deprived them of food and shelter and they were driven out, not to return. Meanwhile, the *Titanic* disaster represented the end of an era of blithe cultural optimism. It now seemed to me even more significant that in Aunty May's telling the ship went down and the birds fell silent together. Not a jeremiad from the fields but a silence, precursor of more silent springs to come. This was April 1912. Two years later the nations of Europe blustered themselves into a war that would destroy millions of lives and homes, and by the fillip it gave to the industrial-technical complex hasten the disenchantment of the subcontinent and the entire world. I no longer question the meaning of Aunty May's story: it is a myth of the mutual dependency of civilized human culture and the natural environment – a myth that it is urgently necessary to recover.

March 2021, and the days were slowly lengthening again. Usually, after our son had gone to sleep, there was still an hour of half-light left, so if I had time to myself, I would sometimes go for a walk down to the beach or beside the stream that runs through the big park, where if you know where to look you can find the levelled remains of two old watermills. Most often, though, poor weather deterred me from walking. On these wet evenings, having left Tommy's room and switched on the landing nightlight, I would pad into the study and either take a book from the shelves or simply stare out of the window at the rows of houses and the bay beyond. There would always be something to interest the eye, whether a crowd of students tottering and shrieking through the rain on their way to town, the nightly congregation of starlings on the cricket ground floodlights, or simply the hide-and-seek of the moon as it tried to see past the rainclouds. I also watched with increasing interest and admiration the efforts of the magpie pair to refit last year's damaged nest for the new breeding season. The birds had been working at it tirelessly since January at least, and we often saw them, as we passed on our way to or from school, swooping down to the road to collect loose sticks, some presumably the same that they had used last year, before the gales had come.

Two years had passed since Grandma's death and the dizzying sense of personal lostness that had accompanied it. Since then, my attempts to think things through had necessarily been halting, but on this particular night I felt again, as I watched the comings and goings of the magpies, that I had made progress of a sort. I was grateful for the little revelations that had come to me over the course of those two years. The period of my shamanic flights back to Eardlem had left me with the insight that objects forlorn of their old context could in theory be integrated purposefully into a new one, much after the manner of these exemplary magpies weaving last year's sticks into a new nest. And my visits to Mum and to my childhood home had helped in many ways, though not necessarily ones I could have foreseen. I had become more conscious that for the greater part of these two years I had desired to cleave tighter to the lost past in the hope of finding an anchorage there, but that the opposite had happened: the cumulative and salutary effect of all that I had learned and felt about Grandma's childhood, Mum's and my own had been to free me from this unhealthy dependence on the past. In two enlightening stages I had realized, first, that it was myself, not Eardlem or the past of any place, that needed to be 'fixed' in Ian Hamilton Finlay's sense, and, second, that the part of me that needed fixing was the part that lives now, in the present. In short, I felt, as the light faded and the magpies retired for the night, that I had learned a lot about where not to look, and about letting go.

I knew now that I disagreed with Alan Garner that 'inheriting one's childhood landscape and growing in it to maturity' is the only way to 'know one's place'. I could see why Garner might have thought so, or needed to think so, but if the dogma was true of other people's experiences at the time he devised it, it surely applied to fewer and fewer people now. In light of this, it might seem paradoxical that this was the very night on which I decided to return to Eardlem. Yet I had been circling round the place for so long, and touched it so many times in my memory and imagination, through Mum's retellings and in Grandma's Red Book, that I felt I could only move on from it, in a healthy way, by seeing it for myself one last time. Besides, for all that I had spent so long, as I now understood, in the wrong relation to Eardlem, it was still the prime cause and emotional centre of everything I had been trying to recover, and to recover *from*. No, it was not Canaan; I knew that now. Though I still had no clear idea where I was going, I knew that I could not go back. But if belonging really is a relationship, as I had come to think, between a person and somewhere or something bigger than themselves, then I could not hope to establish that relationship honestly before I had properly closed my account with Eardlem. Not, of course, that I wanted to forget about it or depreciate its importance in my making. But the past and I needed to be easy with each other again. So I switched my attention from the magpies, opened the laptop and booked tickets north.

9

The village of Eardlem straddles a sandstone ridge close to the border of modern Staffordshire and Cheshire. To the north-east is Mow Cop, the westernmost afterthought of the Pennines; to the north-west the rain-green Cheshire Plain. Due west and distant are the hills and mountains of Wales: the Berwyns, Bryniau Clwyd and, it is said, even Eryri itself. Some time in the early seventh century newcomers arrived here: men, women and children from northern continental Europe. These 'Englisc', as they called themselves, had hitherto in their conquest and settlement of Britain preferred to infiltrate the river system and travel by boat. But though the River Trent rises not far from Eardlem, there is no navigable water near the ridge, so they would have had to reach here instead on foot, on horseback and by wooden chariot and cart. They stopped short of the fertile but indefensible plain and cleared the trees from the ridge. Among them was a woman called Aldge. High-born, she was entitled to own land. She claimed a meadow and in time the place was named after her, though the evolving language obscured the connection. By Domesday the acreage had grown; there was now land for three ploughs, and a wood 'one mile long and one mile wide, worth three shillings'.

The motte erected on the ridge by Aldge and her people is still plainly visible. It was raised against the Christian *Wealas*, or 'Welsh', who defied the Englisc behind the batteries of grey mountains to the west, but the newcomers were fascinated by the people beyond the mountains, and their strange, singing language, something that remains evident in the names of modern Eardlem's new-builds: Plas Newydd, Tŷ Bryn, Y Bwthyn. For centuries the people of Eardlem have looked west, whether in curiosity or fear. It was through the Cheshire Gap that Sir Gawain rode from 'the wyldrenesse of Wyrale' in search of the Green Chapel where he expected to be beheaded by a knight from the Otherworld; three centuries later, a group of Royalist soldiers stained the flagstones of St Bertoline's, in nearby Barthomley, with the blood of villagers who had sought sanctuary in the tower. St Bertoline's, and St James's, Eardlem, were quarried in piety from the ridge, but no niceties were observed when the coal mines slit the hills and spilled out heaps of spoil. It was to Wolstanton Deep Pit that my great-grandfather, John Till – a widower with five children – came queuing for work in the late 1920s, only to be undercut by the boy behind him, who shouted to the clerk that he'd do the job for a shilling less a month. John's children shared a zinc bath, one after the other, and there was often too little food. But he was liked, and prior to the welfare state that could make a material difference. My grandma told me that one day a policeman had come to the door. Little Doris hid behind her father as he answered. The policeman said that in a place they both knew, the door to a rabbit hutch had been left unlocked. The next day, for the first time in weeks, the children had meat.

So much for the past. I have come up on the train to Crewe and nearly died twenty deaths walking the few miles to Eardlem down lanes of reckless traffic, often having to lean backwards into the sulphur-dusted hedges to avoid being struck. I had prepared myself, three years having passed since Grandma's death, and after all the anxious reappraisals that had happened since, to see this once almost-familiar landscape with the disappointed eyes of an outsider, but in the landscape was an even greater desolation than I'd feared. Once, I found a footpath and turned off into fields, yet found them almost empty. Pheasants retched in the odd damp squared-off copse, but otherwise the only birds were crows and buzzards turning listlessly in the foul warm wind raised by the traffic. A cock chaffinch called from an oak, but received no answer.

People don't stop in Eardlem. There's really nothing to do here except live, so it's an Airbnb blackspot. But it's tiring to drive between Birmingham and Manchester, so there's a convenient motel a mile away. This is where I've booked in for the night, with the idea of spending the whole day in Eardlem tomorrow. I don't know what I'd been expecting but of course it makes perfect sense that there should be no footpath to the motel. I'm not going to take my chances as a pedestrian on the slip road, so I improvise a back way that involves trespassing across ploughland brown and sticky as gateau and then pushing arsewise through the thorn bushes that guard the motel precincts from . . . what? Finally I break through and emerge into an oily simoom blowing from the extractor fans of Burger King, yet immediately I step away from it my attention is arrested by something familiar but unexpected. It takes me a second to realize that it is birdsong. The motel grounds are absolutely ringing with it. I stand and count eight species, including nuthatch, mistle thrush and greatspotted woodpecker. It's so unexpected that I feel like laughing. I take my binoculars out from beneath my shirt and am about to scan the trees when a movement catches my eye from beneath the miserable shrubs planted around KFC. A cat? A fox? I raise the binoculars. It's hens. Five fat brown hens nutting the woodchip ten yards from the swinging doors of KFC, each utterly unaware of the other's true purpose. When the CCTV for that day was reviewed, the security guard would have had a treat: first a denim rump worming into shot through the pyracantha and then, a few seconds later, the emergent oddball pointing his binoculars into the bushes and finally buckling with mirth.

When I'd checked in and washed the exhaust fumes from my skin, I opened the laptop on the bed to confirm what by now I strongly suspected. Sure enough, the online map showed that the motel grounds, noosed by roads but thickly planted with trees, were an oasis of cover among the surrounding empty fields. No wonder the place was full of birdsong: I was in Eden.

It felt wrong to halt so close to Eardlem, the place that had been hardly out of my mind this last two summers, but it was too late in the day: everything would be closed and it would be dark by the time I reached Grandma's. But in the half-hour of remaining light I decided to walk the short distance to a place I knew as Brocky Bank, somewhere we had always come to pick black-berries. I wanted to see the Bank, but also to look down from it at the motorway, which had been preoccupying me in a vague but persistent way ever since I had read in the Red Book about Grandma's car journey of 1926, and begun to consider the con-nection between the road system and the decline of Eardlem's civic and natural life.

We used to come up to Eardlem every fortnight, taking either the M6 or the A-road that runs past Lichfield, depending on the radio weather and travel reports. To my sister and me, bicker-ing or listening in the back to Bob Dylan and Dad being Bob Dylan, it mattered little which route we took; our only wish was to avoid the tedium of traffic jams and escape the car as quickly as possible. And of course we never thought to consider when the motorway had been built, nor troubled ourselves over its social and environmental significance. So dull-witted had I always been, and so compartmentalized my thinking, that it was not until a trip to Eardlem in my thirties that the motorway had begun to trouble me and invite me to face its contradictions, and how I was implicated in them. Now, in this summer of 2021, following all the self-examination that had followed Grandma's death at the prompting of my unconscious, I was able to understand that even back then, some years before my crisis on the train, my visits to Eardlem had been at least partly prompted by my disorientation in life, and by the subliminal hope that the village held the key to reconnection.

On one such visit I had left Grandma napping and closed the door quietly behind me. With binoculars and apple I was walking close to the border with Cheshire, daydreaming and, I suppose, composing odd phrases in my head out of the things I could see, as is my habit when alone. This time something was intruding into my thoughts and interfering with whatever rhyme or pretty alliteration I'd been playing with. It was a noise like the droning of a million flies over slurry, and it was coming from the other side of the field, rising up invisibly but evilly from behind a holly hedge. It was, of course, the motorway. I stood listening to it and felt a penny drop that should have landed many years before. I had walked, toddled and been carried through this landscape, off and on, for my whole life but I swear this was the first time I had properly heard the M6 and how it fouled the soundscape. Not by coincidence, there was, of course, little birdsong to be drowned out, but such was the noise from the motorway that it obscured even the low keening of the summer cows newly bereaved of their calves.

And having once heard the motorway, I could never again

unhear it. My grandparents' house was shielded from both sight and sound of it by a low roll of the landscape, but wherever else I walked, unless I deliberately went several miles to the east, I could hear the background drone of the lorries and cars ripping up the stagnant air between Birmingham and Manchester. And I realized that it wasn't even its volume I minded so much, but rather its permanence. Every other sound around me, whether natural in origin or artificial, came and went. But the din of the motorway wasn't deciduous in that way. It did not rise and fall but continued, incessant, unnatural. This was the period in my life when discussion of what we now know as environmental grief was first beginning to enter the mainstream media, and though I tried to protect myself from it I often read, or more often only half-read, newspaper articles about how our lifestyles are complicit in the ecological loss we passively abhor. I hated the motorway then, even as I understood that it had been built precisely to allow the kind of easy journey across the Midlands that not only the optimistic society of the 1960s, but Aldge and her fellow Englisc would have sincerely taken for progress.

When I had returned from the walk, over tea in the sun-filled back room facing the fields I had asked Grandma about her memories of when the motorway was built, and the next Sunday in our weekly phone call I had put the same question to Mum. Though I may be guilty of projecting my more recent thinking onto the past, it seems to me that even then, in listening to them, I had begun to understand the M6 in a new way: not just as a material blight but as a complex metaphor – a concrete metaphor, you might say – capable of making sense of otherwise separate-seeming strands of experience, from the personal to the social and the global. Certainly, I remembered questioning afterwards whether the destruction of the landscape of the

Staffordshire-Cheshire border had been inevitable, and asking myself whether it could ever be reversed. Assuredly it could. It would be a policy decision like any other. Why, then, did the very notion of removing the motorway seem utterly fanciful, less realistic than the prospect of an uninhabitable Earth? Though once again I may have been crediting my younger self with more clarity of thought than I had really possessed, it seemed to me now, in that late afternoon of 2021, on the walk between the motel and Brocky Bank, that even long ago I had dimly sensed a link between that problem and my decades-long failure to even really see, hear and smell the road.

Yes, in retrospect it seemed likely that I had stumbled then upon the same obscurity in my own thinking that I had been working more systematically to remove ever since returning from Ian Hamilton Finlay's garden – an obscurity caused by a failure to make connections between the concrete and the abstract, the private and the global. But by now I had at least some kind of response to the question, which was at the same time an explanation for why the question itself had so long proved elusive. When you meet a blockage like this, that is at the same time illogical and apparently immovable, you are probably up against an ideology, or in other words a story so necessary to maintaining an untruth that it has clotted into a kind of myth. In the case of the M6 there were two mutually reinforcing myths: the familiar capitalist myth of unending growth, and the supporting myth that the first myth has nothing to do with you and is unquestionable. Myths can't be translated into, let alone dislodged by, arguments, but only by other stories, and the bit of research I'd done in my thirties – questioning Mum and Grandma and then spending a few hours in online follow-up – scant as it was, had been enough for me to now tell a counter-story of my own.

One September day in 1962 a woman and her daughter walked out together to pick blackberries. The woman, aged forty-one, was Doris May and you may guess that the twelve-year-old girl was my mother, whose name is Gillian. It was a beautiful day, the sun jammed at noon. As they mounted the stile by the cattle farm – Doris May hitching a long skirt, Gillian bending awkwardly in the flared jeans that had not long been invented – they saw a bright squint of water where the cows drank. I've often walked that way myself. The path is flattish right till the end. The blackberries grow on a hill that used to be a spoil mound from one of the collieries. Everyone knows it as Brockwood Hill, or just Brocky Bank, and I daresay there really were many badgers curled up inside it. The sun-loving bramble bushes grow on the south-west of Brocky Bank, facing across the Cheshire Plain. If you stand there in clear weather you can see the Lovell radio-telescope at Jodrell Bank as a white smudge in the distance, its simpleton's face tilted trustingly to the stars.

By now Doris May (holding a tartan-patterned Thermos of water and two pairs of gardening gloves) and Gillian (holding a nest of Tupperware boxes) have made it to the top of Brocky Bank. There are many bramble patches around Eardlem, but they have chosen the Bank because the berries grow best there, and also because they half-want to see how the motorway is getting on. It already seems to have taken for ever, and after the first few weeks of excitement the children of the village have almost stopped cycling over there and reporting back the progress of the diggers, steamrollers and other machines, many of them larger than the children's own houses. But it's still all over the papers and the wireless, and now Grandad has somehow managed to get hold of a TV set, which they've set up in the front room. They have neither licence nor aerial but he's worked out how to get a signal by balancing a shoe polish tin and a bent coat hanger on top of the set. 'The picture's alright,' he says, 'as long as you don't move a muscle.'

So at six o'clock each evening he and Grandma, Jack and Gill, process in there through the stale reek of Jack's cigarette smoke and kneel down as though for devotions, tuning the shoe polish tin if the picture goes snowy. And emerging through the fog and the snow they see the small, cocksure figure of transport secretary Ernest Marples striding towards them over a newly laid section of motorway, accompanied by a breathless commentary on the newsreel. In suit and tie Marples, 'in the role of the last pedestrian', as the voiceover has it, walks into the future along the empty concrete strip lolled out across the countryside, between a few doomed English elms. Over busy music the newsreel narrator describes the technical achievement of the M6. One machine is capable of laying 2,000 feet of concrete a day. The narrator continues, 'Over the motorway they've built a restaurant, a touch of imagination for which the hungry and thirsty motorists will bless the designers.' He ends by saying, 'They named this motorway M6. Good luck to all who scorch along her.'

Now, as they reach the top of the Bank, Doris May and Gillian take in with their own senses the long strip, grey like an ox tongue, the clatter and groan of the diggers and the smell of tar that carries across the fields to mingle with the familiar sweet tang of muck. They stand there for a while, surprising themselves and the other by their silence; then they set to work blackberrying, not altogether systematically, but just following their eyes to where the clusters seem thickest. There are thorns everywhere, of course, but at least it is still early enough in the year that the brown and white spiders whose webs drape the bushes have not yet swelled to their full horrific size. Both women are slim and deft, adept at angling the hand from shoulder, elbow and wrist to reach into the fissures of the bush for the fattest, glossiest berries. Their gathering separates them as they each pursue real and imagined richness around different bushes, many of which are twice their height.

For two hours they harvested, while the sun crept on its dial and the shapeless shadows of the bushes stalked them across the grass. At the end, like figures emerging from a Swiss clock, their paths again intersected and they met, exhausted, their hands' lifelines purple with juice and small yellow thornlets under their fingernails, and with four Tupperwares of plump purple-black berries, besides the odd rogue red one that, as Doris May remarked 'somehow always gets in'. And then she said to Gillian: 'You know, they're advertising in *The Sentinel* for surveyors on the next section of the motorway. No experience necessary. We could do with a bob or two.' Before the crumble was out of the oven that night, Grandma had answered the advertisement and by the end of the week she had the job.

By the time I was born the Staffordshire section of the M6 was fourteen years old and Ernest Marples had fled to Monte Carlo with the Fraud Office in tepid pursuit, having siphoned off two million pounds through an overseas interest in order to avoid paying tax in the UK. Much of his wealth, it transpired, had come to him through his civil engineering company, to which as Conservative Minister of Transport he awarded many lucrative contracts.

Almost exactly a century before the North Staffs section of the M6 was laid, a young man named Joseph Challinor, who had a local reputation as a poet, took that same track up Brocky Hill and wrote these lines:

Over Brocky Hill the kestrels hover,
O'er the pasture calls a plover,
Larks arise from growing clover,
And sweetly sing.

Nobody would these days think to emulate Challinor, and not
only because nothing rhymes with 'dual carriageway'. Danish
writer Dorthe Nors has summed things up: 'That's civilization
for you, I think. A track becomes a path, the path becomes an old
road, becomes a country road, becomes a main road, becomes
a motorway; but once it's become a motorway it has long since
stopped talking to the landscape.' Like the incomprehension
between the person who settles down on their native acre and
the one who moves to the city, so too do the land and the road
find that they have nothing to say to each other.

So it was that my sister and I were of the first generation of children to experience the British landscape from a motorway. We
went to visit Grandma and Grandad about twice a month, sometimes indeed scorching along but just as often one more static car
in a miles-long line of private vehicles. When we were stuck we
listened to cassette tape compilations made by my dad, played
necessarily quite limited games of 'I spy', competed in counting
cars of a particular colour – since this was the 1980s, there were
many wonderful, now obsolete, colours, from radish through
cinnabar to uncooked mince – and made words out of the letters
on numberplates. We were at least using our brains. Sometimes
we also counted kestrels, which alone of the species named by
Joseph Challinor had adapted to the motorway. Even when
everyone else had lost interest, I kept a back-seat tally of these
handsome little falcons, twisting my neck around to keep them

in sight for a second or two longer as they hovered, seemingly untroubled by the noise and foul air buffeting up from the traffic. I was as riveted by them as they were on the mice and voles that I imagined assembling in quaking legions at the roadside. It didn't occur to us that our means of accessing the countryside was also killing it, even as we remarked on the animal corpses at the road-side. Back then I had eyes only for the kestrels, and couldn't see how, in the end, their flourishing and ours are entwined.

10

The next morning I set off for Eardlem with a shrink-wrapped sandwich from the petrol station fridge. Finally, I would see it again. I was aware of thinking and feeling nothing. It was the same blankness I'd experienced on the train ride to the nursing home, just over two years before. The same unconscious defence against what I might find.

From the west you enter the village by crossing the motorway bridge and then following the lane down and round past the cricket ground. Then you rise up the hill that made the place so attractive to Aldge and her people, taking a narrow road between terraced houses of blue-brown Potteries brick. Someone is outside washing his car, and he nods me a greeting. The air smells faintly of chimney smoke, as it always did. An agitated blackbird jets between two houses and disappears over the hedge like a hearse equipped with a klaxon. A soapy rope of water slips off the kerb and rolls down the hill as I climb the opposite way.

At the top of the lane I stand panting almost opposite the dim sandstone porch of St James the Great, where my parents were married. I peer into it, trying too hard, as I understand now, to force the past to make me feel something. Suddenly I am aware of feeling lonely, and I wish that my wife and children were here with me. What, in the end, am I really doing here, so far away from them? I picture my son's face as it had looked when he waved me off the previous day. From the church I go to look at the theatre where both of my grandparents acted, and then next door to the library, where I put down my rucksack in front of the local history section. The librarian is helpful: 'Are you looking for anything in particular?' I say that I'm looking for the past. 'Aren't we all, duck.'

If anything is to be redeemed from this lost and disenchanted world of ours, and if our futures are to be fed by our collective past, then the local history shelves of branch libraries must become as precious to us as clean water and clean air. Still impatient at first, after a while, and as I leafed through books about old Eardlem, I felt my restless mind and time itself slow down. I was not grasping for meaning anymore; meaning swam up out of the pages to meet me.

A couple of the local history books I'd pulled out combined factual information with the first-person reminiscences of people who had been born and raised in the village. Always it was community that was emphasized. 'A whole host of traditions,' I read, 'were linked with the local chapels.' At a time when it was rare for Eardlem people even to visit the British coast, let alone travel abroad, the holiday highlight of the year was Wakes Week. In a cupboard back in Swansea, I had a typewritten poem about the Wakes, written by Grandad, part of a series of poems he'd entitled 'Recollections of Boyhood'. In the Wakes poem, Grandad describes his excitement as, with two pennies closed in his fist, he follows the sound of organ music to the fairground, and is caught in two minds whether to spend them on an ice cream or the coconut shy. In the end he cannot resist the painted wooden 'dobby horses' of the carousel:

Round and round, and up and down,
The music swelling in my ears.

I was alive and at the 'wakes'!
Could there be more to life than this?

I opened another book and read more boyhood recollections, from a slightly older contemporary of Grandad's:

In my youth, Mill Dale was teeming with children on Good Friday with their hot cross buns and lemonade. Nowadays it is practically deserted. They seem to be attracted by more sophisticated pleasures!

There was one book that sought to trace Eardlem's past back into prehistory. I read about the forests of the Carboniferous, some of whose severed trunks were discovered in the new ploughland created to feed the population during the Second World War, and also during the scouring of the land's surface to make way for the M6. I learned about the area's archaeology. The finds were scant, but enough to suggest human habitation 10,000 years before the coming of the Englisc. A dog walker had come upon a Bronze Age dagger squirming out of a hillside, and two burial sites of the Beaker Folk are surmised. Better attested is the Roman garrison at Chesterton, built to subdue the Celtic Cornovii from whom I have often imagined I descend.

Some of the Roman artefacts from Chesterton were discovered during the literal descents undertaken by the miners of the Apedale Colliery, among them at least two of my forebears. In the mid 1980s we drove to Chesterton regularly to play crown green bowls, and for some reason I have retained those memories of bowling very clearly. Whenever I wish, in my mind's eye I can still see my parents and grandparents standing or bending to the heavy black balls on the green, which is severed from the surrounding darkness of forgetting as though the green were one of dad's square slides held up to the light. But their figures stand upright and cast shadows, like 3D cut-outs on the surface, and as if they were attached to the torsos by those golden split paper fasteners we used at school, their arms as they cast the bowls swing back and forth, back and forth. At our house in Swansea, in the understairs cupboard, my grandad's two bowls and the smaller jack still sleep in their leather case, like crocus bulbs in the dark earth, awaiting a new spring.

After an hour in the library I close the books, feeling a little drunk on the past and that things are in danger of turning maudlin. Under the circumstances it's probably not the best time to force my feet through the village and then down the avenue to take a look at my grandparents' house, but after all, I don't know whether I will ever be here again. The sun stands high and shines down blandly on the Patch, the green opposite their house on which, as I know from Mum, in past decades there used to be huge November bonfires. I come to the house and note numbly that the front garden has gone, replaced with a drive. But the house looks the same. I tell myself that it *is* the same. Someone else lives in it now, that's all. Under the rasp and wheeze of young starlings calling from the trees I turn away and walk to the end of the avenue, where I face the fields so that only the cows will see my weeping. Over their metal water-trough and the ragged hedge a single swallow comes skimming for insects. Sometimes it's difficult to be sure what you weep for. People these days carry so much, and weep so seldom, damming a million tears. But I know what I weep for. I weep for the days when Grandma would wave us off at the gate, and because I shall not see her again.

Weary of the traffic jams, having thought of every animal beginning with Z, hungry and impatient to see Grandma, we all craned forwards at the turn-off for Eardlem as though doing so would give the car a final spurt. Having left the motorway behind, we could all enjoy the semi-illusion that we were now in the countryside. A farm passed us to the right, smelling of sweet silage, and on the left we glimpsed through a five-bar gate the little hollow of oaks where someone had tied a rope-swing over a shallow brook and Grandad once told us that he had played cowboys and Indians as a lad. We passed the pub, the Bargain Booze that retails oatcakes, the memorial obelisk surrounded by plastic poppy wreaths and then the sandstone church with its steps speckled with colourful plastic confetti, through the village and then finally down the long avenue to Grandma's house with its sacred prospect over the fields.

The car stops and 'The House of the Rising Sun' is silenced mid arpeggio. We pivot stiff-legged from the back seat, brushing biscuit crumbs from trouser legs, and instead of the staleness of the car interior comes the cool sweet smell of the grass that has just been mown on the Patch. The smell of Eardlem is this cut grass, chimney smoke and cow muck, it is the smell of not-Birmingham, the smell of Away. In this present foray into the past, time has been mashed together. Dad still has his 1970s facial fuzz and Buddy Holly glasses, but Mum has a toppling 1980s perm, like an unstable, ambitious meringue. My sister has pebbly spectacles and wears a tartan dress, though I know this isn't a true memory but one taken from a photograph I have in my desk drawer at home in Swansea.

Below the Patch a wooden gate on a mulish metal latch separates the garden path from the avenue. The path curves to the front door, past the passage between houses which in this part of the country is called an 'entry', and around a small lawn with its centre dug out to host a blowsy, brown-mottled hydrangea. In summer we would lurch through the dim, brick-and-bacon smelling entry, slopping water from brim-full watering cans to darken the soil around the flowers. Marigolds, pansies and a few roses circle the hydrangea, but on the far side, instead of flowers, thorn bushes have been planted against the neighbouring Liberal Democrats.

My sister and I have reached grandma's front door. Sometimes she will have been looking out for us, in which case even from the car we may have caught sight of her, silhouetted behind the net curtains in the front room. But if she's in the back cooking then we'll have to ring the bell. As though it were happening in front of me, I watch as Grandma's form assembles itself in pastel blotches swimming out of the hall through the marbled glass door. When she opens the door a smell of roast chicken will steam out. There'll be no embraces, and if traffic has made us more than a bit late she'll ask in relieved exasperation where we've been and inform us that the vegetables have been ready for the last half hour.

But there'll be smiles for my sister and me, and we'll walk, still limping from our confinement in the car, down the thickly carpeted hall, past the stand for walking sticks. Some of these, the pale ones with curved ends like shepherds' crooks, were shop-bought, but most were made by distant relatives and one of them, short, dark and knobbed, can only have been passed down the generations from a genuine Wildman of the Woods. We would have liked to fence with these sticks, but the hall being narrow, and the elders opposed, the bouts are immediately snuffed out and I have to be content with grimacing, armed, in front of the hall mirror. The hall is a clamour of our Brummie accents, which haven't yet been lost to grammar school and university.

Our coats and shoes go into the understairs cupboard, cluttered and smelling of polish and leather. In the furthest darkness is the cramped spot where we crouch and try to silence our hot, busy bodies during games of hide and seek. For a small house there are surprisingly many hiding places, the most popular of which, even when it became too obvious through overuse, was the huge oaken ottoman on the landing. One of the few beautiful pieces of furniture in the house, it held layers of linen and blankets of coarse wool that would cause you to itch all night if you had the misfortune to lie under one. These various fabrics all but filled the ottoman, so when you climbed in you had to flatten yourself like a hare in its form in order that the lid would properly close – and gently, mind, lest the seeker hear the giveaway thud. There in the softness and darkness you would stay, excited and happy. If the seeker's footsteps faded into another room, by humping back and shoulders you could raise the lid just a little to admit air and see dust motes falling like meteors in the shafts of light that fell through the small landing skylight.

We follow Grandma through to the living room with its paperweights, clocks and calendar of common garden birds. A stoneware dish of sweating butter rests on the carpet in front of the gas fire's metal grille. On top of the fire itself is a small brass bell crowned by the smirking effigy of a Cornish imp. My sister and I were fascinated by this bell, which is another one of the treasured effects of that house to have come down to me, and we were always drawn to glide our fingers over the satisfying shape of the imp, from his head to the bulge of the knees that were drawn up beneath his chin. I never saw anyone else move it, except Grandma when she dusted, but my sister and I rang and rang it until the small grimy clapper got jammed on the inside of the bell or one of the adults shouted from the kitchen for us to 'pipe down'.

Grandma has already returned to her station in the kitchen, warily accommodating of the sous chef, my mother. In this scene I can't picture Dad, who may still be processing stoically back and forth from the open car boot with our luggage. But our attention is drawn to the wide windows at the back of the room for *there* is the wide beloved view onto the fields, muddied by the constant traffic of cattle, barely divided by the hedges they have dismantled. Our eyes sweep the fields and then ascend the slope of Kent Hills to the mysterious little rectangular building that caps the underground reservoir. Out of the nearer distance comes a stiff-winged and jocular rabble of starlings flying from the fields towards us. Just beyond the window is a shanty of bird feeders with rain-sodden seed slopping out of plastic dishes, and cages of balled fat swaying from iron hooks. Grandma and Grandad love birds, and on the outhouse wall either Grandad or my father has fixed a bird box that some years is found acceptable to blue tits. Much later, when I visit Grandma alone, it will sometimes be my duty to remove the old nest, an office I perform in terror lest, with the fledgelings now gone, spiders have moved in. Or worse, that one of the chicks has perished, and that I'll prise the lid to find its crawling, huge-headed corpse, eyes still sealed shut that have never seen the sun.

When we were younger we played upstairs at drawing or dressing up, and at Christmas we gathered around the plastic tree in Jack's room at the front, but otherwise almost all of the time we spent in Eardlem was in this light-filled room at the back, from which we could watch the broken floes of clouds being drawn like newsprint through a press, over hill and under heaven from their ultimate origin in the Irish Sea. It would be strange if all the time I spent looking at this vista, which must amount in sum to weeks or even months of my life, had not left a lasting imprint in my mind's eye, and indeed in these recollections, even as at the time, I'm aware of having to make an effort to turn my head and drag my attention back to the room, its activities and fixtures. It is presumably also my long habit of gazing at these objectively quite unremarkable fields, and the motley of cloud and light passing over them, that has fixed them in my nostalgia as the quintessence of what I have lost.

I am at that window now, seven years old, forehead pressed against the glass. Mum's voice comes out of the dimness behind me, telling me to sit up because I'm smudging the pane. I turn around. 'Why don't you draw something?' She is gesturing to one of the dark wooden sideboards from which my sister, now in her toddling era and wearing a white woollen cardigan knit-ted by Grandma, has already pulled down the hinged shelf of the bureau and is firking around inside. The cupboard space is filled with stationery and all the effects and ephemera of the pre-digital writer: A4 paper lined or blank, with sometimes a pad of trans-lucent tracing paper. Old toffee and biscuit tins, some bearing sentimental images of Venice or one of the Dorset castles, rattle with paperclips, bulldog clips, treasury tags, pencil sharpeners and thick, lead-, titanium- and mintcake-coloured erasers which, although scuffed white and flaking at the corners, never seemed to wear down. There are loose biros whose lids we must not chew, and packeted rows of felt-tipped pens whose lids we must not forget to replace.

When we had made our selection we'd go back to the dining table under the window, one leg having been dragged out to leave a dark wake through the carpet fibres, and one of its leaves unfolded. This was the same table on which we played Scrabble, Battleships or Stop-the-Bus, and every day we shared round the concise crossword, leaving the cryptic one for Grandma. She'd come back in from the kitchen having had a brainwave, and explain with a flourish of her finger or a biro how the clue was solved. Then from our opposite sides of the table, we would fill the mortified hour before lunch by drawing animals, maps, dragons, aerial dogfights or spaceships. The images came 'from our heads' but were naturally much influenced by whichever books were then in vogue with us, whether Spot the Dog, Percy Trezise and Dick Roughsey's superb tales of those Australian spirits called Quinkins, or later, inevitably, the landscapes and inhabitants of Middle-earth, whose milder regions were, as we later discovered, based on Tolkien's memories of his own childhood enchanted ground in the West Midlands, not so very far from Eardlem. If tracing paper was available, I would lay it down on Grandad's field guide to British birds and carefully go round the shapes of lapwings, corncrakes, yellowhammers – unaware then that a generation earlier these were all birds I could have seen from the window.

The artists were kept replenished, as artists should be, with strong tea in mugs factory-painted with wildflowers, but it was difficult to rise or return or even to cross your legs under the table without knocking the tabletop and causing milky tea to slop over the edge of the mug. Most often the table would be upset by someone trying to open the sideboard drawers that held tablecloths, woven mats and cutlery. The cutlery was of an old kind you don't see now: small with black-mottled metal blades and plastic handles of mock ivory. To the left of the drawers, and below a glass-fronted recess containing ugly green Carlton ware, was a dark cupboard behind sliding wooden doors that contained playing cards and a set of dominoes, black with a lizard design, in a wooden box made by Grandad. We played 'dommies' and cards for hours, weeks, years, while in the kitchen the vegetables bubbled, Mum and Grandma bickered and sang, and beyond the window downpours of starlings would descend for the suet exclusively bought for the robin, and rainclouds from distant Eryri crept over the Kent Hills to replenish the bird bath. Grandma would go to the garden then to fetch in the washing and loudly berate the starlings.

How I wish she were there now, and all of us together again for the grand homecoming that will never take place. I would like to hear her sing again, as she would still sometimes do, in the later years when I would return by train, alone, to visit her. In my memory the room is dim, though it is only afternoon. It must be winter, very nearly. Time to put the clocks back. Or forwards? I've never known or understood. Grandma's voice calls from the kitchen, asking me to draw the curtains, so I stand up on one of the chairs to pull the folds of dusty cloth across from the top. They never used to be dusty. Grandma comes into the room while I'm doing it and I glance down to see her cradling the upside-down carriage clock. As I climb down from the chair she says, to the clock, 'You shouldn't wind them backwards, you see. I wind it forwards eleven hours. Otherwise you're spoiling the mechanism.' Ah, that's it, then. 'Here you are. You wind this one.' Why does a person need two clocks! As I feel with my finger for the little plastic cog I glance out of the window at the fields I have known all my life. I have drawn and painted them from my first crayon scribbles, scanned them with Grandad's cracked binoculars until I had red rings round my eyes like flying goggles, and sat outside on summer nights to watch them from the outhouse roof, while the moonlight curdled in the tall thistle heads and the Friesians' white blotches floated by in serene, surreal floes, in a rhythm out of time.

'We're doing this for the farmers, you know! But I don't suppose that lazy bugger Price gets out of bed before ten o'clock.' Price is the farmer who owns the fields, but he's no good. He's let the milking barn go to ruin, he won't come for an injured cow, and he hasn't minded the field for years – hence the thistles. Though I've never lived here, I know the history of the farm's ownership going back nearly a century. The further back you go, the more far-fetched are the stories, until you get to Billy Proudlove, whose bull dropped dead one Sunday morning when Proudlove scoffed at the vicar's warning to attend church. The older people's memories here go back into myth like roots into water.

Soon after my visit to Eardlem the school holidays ended and the busy autumn term began at work. The months slipped through our fingers, but in the rare opportunities for reflection I understood that seeing Eardlem again had helped in both of the ways I'd hoped for. In an immediate sense it had given me what is called 'closure'. Yet, by confirming both that I really had belonged to and been fed by the place, but could not expect to re-root myself there again in the present, I sensed that it also marked the completion of the first part of the task suggested to me by the dream-beasts. In the more than two years that had passed since Grandma's death, the network of cracks linking that loss to the weight of unacknowledged grief for a culture in decline and a world in crisis had, if anything, expanded. The sheer emotional difficulty of acknowledging the damage inflicted on the Earth even during my childhood, and the loss of innocence that entailed, combined with my new understanding of the M6 as emblematic of the contradictions and complicities involved in the Great Acceleration, had been necessary medicine to free me from false hope, whether in the past or present. As for the prospect ahead, well, greed and denial, too, had not been idle during the past two years, and the lane to the land of the dead had widened until it seemed almost a motorway itself – one that we seem guaranteed to scorch along.

Acceptance of all this grim knowledge was necessary if I were to find a new place to belong, somewhere to fix myself so that I could place everything else, so that I would cease to feel like an isolated piece of wreckage. The two metaphors of my fissured mind and of myself as poor pilgrim never ceased to be of practical value to me. I've never needed to be persuaded of the great visioning powers of metaphor, but here was an example in my own life of how images can do work beyond the reach of reason.

And they gave me hope. The gifts of insight gained from the Eardlem objects, from my mental journeys to the Eardlem of the past and to my own childhood, from my conversations with Mum and most recently from my visit to the village itself, had enabled me to see that the processes of fragmentation and homelessness that we wreak upon ourselves are, in principle, reversible. A fissure may also be a footpath, a crack, a connection. And the strangest comfort I had taken from the last two years was that in fact it isn't the world of the past that is lost, but our contemporary world, and that if we wish to be easy again with the past then there is no other way to do so than by restoring the present.

Such were my thoughts as I sat at my desk in the study and looked far out across the ocean, where at sunset, backlit, individual fields can sometimes be seen wet and shining behind the cliffs of the north Devon coastline. I had learned that it is necessary to avoid idealizations, and necessary, too, to find continuities between past and present, as painful as these might prove to be. Now I needed to use this knowledge. I hadn't got much more than a collection of metaphors, but, like I say, metaphors are powerful. I could see the labyrinth. I was holding the clew. It was time to set off and try and establish my belonging, 'find myself' in the present.

Part II

'Even as a child I could not look at a bird or a last summer's leaf and say "This hasn't anything to do with me".'

– Margiad Evans

11

The crisis I suffered on that train journey between Bristol and Bath, back in 2017, had given a final impetus to an action we had long been considering, and in August of that year we left Bristol for Swansea. I and our daughters were born in England, my wife is from Hungary, but our son, Thomas, was born here in Wales, six weeks after the move. Moving was the right decision. Before we came I had felt so anxious and unsettled that it was making me ill. I think I didn't really know where I was or where I was *supposed* to be, and the boundedness of Wales helped with that immediately. I don't only mean that it is a smaller country, or that its culture is more successful than the English at making sense of its present by reference to tradition, though these things are true and later came to be better understood and more consciously important for me. In the beginning it was simpler than that.

From the first weeks after we arrived, at first alone and then later often with Tom strapped snoring to my chest, when the weather was clear I liked to walk up the steep streets and through the disused quarry that supplied the stone for so many of the local houses, up and further up on a new footpath meandering between gorse-grown former workings, until I reached the housing estate that caps the hilltop overlooking Swansea Bay. From a bench up there, which in its panoptical position suggests the fo'c'sle of a ship, you can take in forty or more miles of coast, and beyond the mind-calming relief of the view itself, and the beauty of the constant exchange of colours between ocean and sky, I found pleasure in simply tracing this coastline with my eyes, west to east, from the great knuckle of the Gower peninsular, past the spurting orange flame of the steelworks at Port Talbot to the vast dune systems of Cynffig, half obscured in haze.

Most simply of all, though, I loved to see with my own eyes that up here I am at the edge of the land, where the land stops. That is comforting in itself, like choosing a seat from which you can keep an eye on the exit, and it always recalls the sensation of spaciousness I experienced when I first moved to Swansea directly from London, years before during a short-lived earlier residence. Then I had experienced a great feeling of freedom, as though Swansea were the larger city. I mean psychologically larger, of course, and in seeking to explain this I had discovered that it was precisely Swansea's boundedness that gave rise to the freedom. It was like the freedom those avant-garde writers must have felt when, having first rejected grammar and for years flailed miserably in inanities, they recanted and rediscovered the boundless freedom that limits confer.

In the months following Grandma's death I used to come up here to try to sort out my feelings about Eardlem, and by force of habit it was to this bench that I climbed again shortly after my final visit to the village. I was now quite sure that from the time I had first been made aware by Ian Hamilton Finlay's axiom of the nature and extent of my anxiety – that sense of physical, mental and social displacement that had haunted me for years, perhaps even decades – I had been looking for help in the wrong place and the wrong time. Although I had been right to think that it was I who needed to be 'fixed' in order that I could make sense of my life and see myself in the proper relation, my mistake had been to ask too much of Eardlem, or rather to look for too much of myself there. For while all along I had known rationally that I could never really belong in Eardlem, in the confusion of feelings following the funeral, this knowledge had been obscured by my mourning and my haste to find something I could hold on to. I missed Grandma, missed Grandad, missed the house and village and the life of my family and my own past life that had once belonged there. Yes, I missed my childhood, and to look back on it from middle age and parenthood was itself a shock. Loneliness was undoubtedly a part of this too. In middle age you become aware of belonging to a generation, of having contemporaries. Whatever private transports you may experience in your life, you have also been travelling all the time, as you now realize, on a dimly lit night-bus between bright depot and dark terminus. Grasping this, you might then start to fret about the obligations you perhaps owe to your fellow passengers, however anonymous or uncongenial you may imagine them to be.

Moreover, the force of all these interlinked griefs and anxieties had depleted my mental defences against all the other kinds of mourning that I had long fought shy of acknowledging directly: I mourned carefreeness, I mourned my old assumption that the purity of the world could survive exploitative onslaught and I mourned that the literate social democracy I had been born into was now almost dead of neglect. I mourned what I saw everywhere and daily as the passing away of beauty, of probity and civilizing inhibitions, beautiful and shy.

In short, to my natural mourning for a beloved person had latterly been added many less articulable burdens, and they had become confused. Not that I regretted anything: my imaginative flights back to the Eardlem of the past had, as I had long recognized, themselves been a modest form of healing, my conversations with Mum had set a healthy precedent by breaching some of our family's ingrained reticence, and above all, the tears I had shed in Eardlem had enabled me at last to differentiate between the straightforward sorrow for Grandma and the problems of my own lostness. I could see now that though these were certainly related, they were not identical.

All of this brought clarity, and having worked things through so far, in this winter of 2021 I felt for the first time that I should allow the past to fade out in the natural way, to stop gnawing at it, and the idea came more forcefully that I would need to root myself instead in the present. But, just as I was mentally preparing to leave Eardlem behind me, there was a surprise in store. One Sunday morning as I sat on that same bench overlooking Swansea Bay, the phone in my pocket vibrated and a text message came through from my dad.

For years, though intermittently, Dad had been researching the family tree and had compiled hard and electronic versions for my sister and me. Sometimes, while looking for old tax returns or bank statements, I'd come across the folder of paper records, or the digital versions on a USB stick, and take a quick look. I knew, roughly, that both my paternal and maternal ancestors had been manual labourers, mostly miners but also agricultural workers. And it seemed established fact that while Mum's side of the family were all from Eardlem or thereabouts, Dad's family hailed from County Durham and from Tyneside, where he himself was born in 1950. But dad had recently paid to access earlier census records, and what they revealed turned our understanding of our family on its head.

We learned that my great-great grandfather, Thomas Lovatt, was not born in the north-east of England but, of all places, in north Staffordshire. This was in 1790. His place of birth was given as Goldenhill, just five miles east of Eardlem. Accompanying the birth record for Thomas was enough detail, enough 'colour', to bring him and his times to life. His given occupation was a carter, a job which eventually killed him when a spooked horse splintered his ribcage against the cart shaft. But the criminal registers also state that in 1833 he was convicted of larceny and sentenced to seven years' transportation, though it seems the sentence must have been commuted. Even this revelation was eclipsed, though, when Dad accessed the marriage records. In 1811, at the age of twenty-one, Thomas had married Mary Yearsley. They married in the church of St James the Great, in Eardlem, the same church in which my parents were married 161 years later. The coincidence was so unexpected, and so *precise*, that I just laughed. Dad's great-grandfather, whom everyone had assumed to be a Geordie, was born within five miles of where my mum's family came from, and married in Eardlem.

I left the bench and paced around, rereading the message several times over. And I thought first of the time, six months earlier, when I had stood to catch my breath at the top of the hill up to Eardlem village and looked at the sandstone porch of St James's. I remembered how I had striven to sense a bond across time, something that would make me feel I belonged to the place where my parents had been married. And I recalled how I had failed, how the feeling had not come. Knowing now that both sides of my family had been united in that same church, that the wrinkled porch with its inner darkness was, as it were, the family navel, made my failure to wring feeling from it all the more decisive. And I was certain that even if I had stood before the church in the knowledge that my unfortunate forebear Thomas had married there, my pang would still have been for his namesake, my own four-year-old son, who I had so missed while travelling. And I knew that this was as it should be.

But for all that, this discovery of Dad's was no small thing. I think if the text message had arrived a year earlier I would have found it fascinating but frustrating. When I was still mistakenly trying to fix my present identity in Eardlem, the knowledge that both sides of my family were rooted there would have been no comfort because I would only have worried more about what I thought I ought to feel there. By now, though, I had sufficient perspective on where I had been going wrong to take something different from the information. I could see that for my present purposes the practical benefit of Dad's research was not the knowledge that my paternal and maternal lines converged in Eardlem, but precisely that Dad's side had left it and put down roots elsewhere, regrafting the family tree.

The following evening I opened the laptop and tried to fit what Dad had learned about our ancestors, Thomas and Mary Lovatt, into a bigger picture of working-class displacement. I soon discovered that the internal migration of the Lovatts, far from being unusual, had been very common. Perhaps like most people, I had always previously assumed that while the middle class is mobile, the working class is 'rooted' in a particular landscape, whether rural or urban. This, like all myths, is powerful enough to override abundant evidence to the contrary. It wasn't as though I'd never heard of the forced evictions of the Acts of Enclosure or the Highland Clearances, and I remembered having learned at school about the mass economic migrations that accompanied the industrialization of the British economy. But often it isn't until knowledge becomes personal that you regard it properly. This ancestor of mine, Thomas Lovatt, may have been a carter, but one of his sons had been an ironworker and the other a coal miner. In the wake of Dad's message I began to research the economic depression that had affected the formerly thriving coalfield and associated ironworks of the north-west Midlands from the 1860s onwards, and the ensuing unemployment that had sometimes prompted whole factories to uproot themselves fifty miles or more, and their workforces with them. If the rich coal seams were too far away, then the people had had to move anyway, in the hope that they would be taken on once they arrived, and that everything else – a home, food, an education, friends – would follow in time.

Once I discovered that this had happened in my own family, I tried to imagine the personal transformations it would quickly have entailed, particularly those small adjustments that escape the historical record. Dad's grandmother may already have spoken with a similar Geordie accent to his, but *her* father would have spoken in the dialect and accent of the Potteries. 'Cost kick a bo agen a wo, yed it back an bost it?' He moved, presumably by steam train, sometime between the founding of Stoke City FC in 1863 and the establishment of Port Vale FC thirteen years later. If he had indeed been a football fan, he would have had to wait until 1892 for Newcastle United to be created. Four generations later, my dad, who grew up supporting Newcastle, after forty or more years living and working in Birmingham is an Aston Villa fan, a foible my stepmother tolerates with compassion because she knows he can't help it.

Now I found myself wondering with renewed curiosity about Dad's own reaction to the revelation of all this uprooting, and of his relationship to his own roots. Born in South Shields, with his family he had been transplanted to Gloucester in the early 1960s, following his father's new job. Then as an adult he had moved to Birmingham and remained there until 2007, when he had married my stepmother and moved back to within a few miles of his birthplace. What was it like, I wanted to know, to return to one's roots?

12

'My life feels like a jigsaw puzzle,' says Dad. 'But it's only recently that I've been able to see how the pieces have fitted together.' It is February 2022. I came up to Newcastle yesterday, on a train that passed through Birmingham and within ten miles of Eardlem. Now we're walking with binoculars, telescope and a handheld sound recorder along the edge of a field in Holywell, Northumberland, a short way from the house where Dad lives with Val, my stepmother. The landscape is flat and open, the rough pasture sodden and gleaming. Above it the sky, out of which almost every weather you can name will soon fall, is steep and vast and coloured unmistakeably by the reflected light and silence of the ocean. The North Sea is invisible a couple of miles to the east, but sea-light is everywhere, giving the hedgerows and bald spinneys a hybrid, maritime air. The effect is familiar from back home in south Wales, but this North Sea light is deeper, whiter and more austere than that thrown back from the silty Severn Sea. Through the hedge's thorn lattice on our left we see chinks of water shining from Holywell pond. The hedge itself is threaded with the sounds and movements of small birds; in five minutes we see as many species of finch, blue- and great titmice, reed buntings, yellowhammers and an affable yeomanry of tree sparrows. It's partly the birds that have brought us here, but the sound-recording device is intended not for them but for the conversation I'm hoping to have with Dad. We're probably both a little nervous. We don't see each other as often as we'd like, and as I've said we're not a family for talking. It's good, then, that we have this teeming, light-drenched and bird-busy land-scape as a way to get round to it.

Dad pauses and points out a tall stone obelisk off to the right, which in local memory marks the spot where the landowner, Admiral George Delaval, died after being thrown from his horse. A little further off, less than a mile to the south and partly concealed by trees, we can see the tower of St Alban's church, Earsdon. In the churchyard is another, much smaller, monument to the lives of 204 men and boys who were killed on 16 January 1862 when the wooden beam of a pumping engine snapped and thundered down the main shaft of Hartley Colliery, blocking all escape or attempted

rescue behind tons of debris dislodged by its fall. Two men, William Shape and Ralph Robinson, who had been in the colliery cage when the beam fell, were recovered alive in a rope sling lowered from the surface. But thereafter it took a week for rescuers to get past the blockage. Not only rubble but deadly exhalations of carbon monoxide prevented access to the main workings. On the surface the families waited. Days passed – winter days of brittle light as clear as glass. An inquest was prepared. There was a telegram of condolence from the Queen.

When finally the downfall was breached and, themselves dizzied and choking from the gas, the first of the would-be rescuers reached the pit face, their torches lit up heap upon heap of bodies. As it was reported in the next morning's *Shields Gazette*: 'The exploring parties have seen little boys in the arms of their fathers, and brothers sleeping dead in the arms of brothers.' The youngest miner was ten years old. In 200 homes leased from the mine-owners the light of winter coming in at windows fell on the possessions of those who would not come home. The meals prepared by the wives, sisters and daughters of the fore-shift would not be eaten. The tin baths would not be filled. The beam had broken at the worst possible time, as the early-morning shift was preparing to be relieved by the next. From a notebook found in the pocket of one of the dead, detailing a session of prayer, it was surmised that none of the miners had lived beyond Saturday, after spending their final two days in darkness. A mile above them, the hedges were full of the calls of small birds, many more than today. This is a limestone landscape, scooped and riddled by water. It takes its name from a spring, the holy well, dedicated to Mary the mother of God, but from the Middle Ages, when the first shallow shafts were sunk, to the disaster of 1862, the battle was always to keep the sea from surging into the tunnels. In their last hours, a mile or more beneath the ground, the miners would have heard the North Sea as a deep, throbbing boom. And above it their prayers to Mary, still familiar to me from primary school:

ora pro nobis . . .
nunc et in hora ortis nostrae

In the end, the bodies of all the Hartley miners were recovered. But in other pits, nearby and further afield, exhumation was not always possible. Certainly hundreds, possibly thousands of men and children never found their way back up to the cackle of geese and the sea-light on the fields.

A fortnight later, back in Swansea, I would come upon a reminiscence of a woman who lost a brother in the disaster. At a distance of thirty years she was interviewed for the local press:

'There were so many funerals — sometimes four in one day.' She smiles as she remembers how her younger brother and his friend even played at funerals indoors. 'We'd take the long horse-hair cushion from the sofa and lay it across two chairs. That represented the coffin. Then we put Dad's cap and our school hats on the cushion. They were the wreaths.' Her brother would stand at one end of the cushion — his friends at the other, both wearing their caps. They would solemnly remove these while they sang 'Rock of Ages'.

There is no need to go digging for the past. We carry it inside us always. And sometimes, in those rare and most private moments when our souls are receptive and our superficial, practical identities are taken by surprise, all it takes is a little new knowledge, or the mysterious surfacing of a long-buried memory, for us to feel that our very constitutions and sense of selfhood are suddenly vulnerable to flooding by the past. So rapid and complete can this inundation be that we may feel in uncanny moments that it is not the past but rather the present that is distant and somehow ungraspable. This very lake that we're now looking onto, with its shining black skin and rafts of winter duck, is a flooded mineworking. Dad and I have been walking less than an hour but already the trivial morning has been broken open from beneath by what we would ordinarily call coincidences. Some are unremarkable in themselves, such as that my paternal grandfather, like George Delaval, was in the navy, and that in a few weeks Dad will begin a birdwatching holiday by flying to Málaga, site of the naval battle that made the admiral's name. But what to make of the likelihood, later confirmed by research, that Hartley Colliery was one of those that drew mineworkers and their families from the north-west Midlands? Census records from the late nineteenth century disclose a steady trickle of Lovatts to precisely the area we're now walking. Even as we follow these footpaths in the bright morning, chatting and directing each other's attention to the appearance and immediate presence of birds, light, clouds – all the time it is as though we are being sounded from below, as though the past were suddenly very near.

In June 1892 my great-grandfather Joseph was the first of the Lovatts to be born in the north-east. His father, another Thomas, who had been born near Eardlem in 1865, by the time of the 1881 census was living in a terrace house in South Shields, purpose-built for the miners of the Harton Colliery, which is just twelve miles south of Hartley, where we are now walking. In Hartley Thomas courted a local young woman named Annie Harrison, and when he was twenty-seven and she twenty-two they gave birth to Joseph, who at the age of eleven followed his father underground, where in due course he lost an eye and then broke his leg in an accident of 1921, the same year in which, back in north Staffordshire, my maternal grandmother Doris May Till of Eardlem was born. Then, again according to the *Gazette*, in 1922 Joseph was buried under a fall of stones and lay immobile, along with three other miners, for thirty hours. He survived, but with crushing injuries to his chest and legs that left him all but unable to walk for the next six months. By this time Joseph had been married to Ethel May Rennie for the last decade, and one of their six children was my dad's father, of whom in this mixture of sunshine, wind and hail, Dad is now speaking with a tremor in his voice.

We have passed Holywell pond and are at a corner where four fields meet. We are in our element. We point out birds to each other, sometimes asking each other for confirmation. A male kestrel in a smoke-blue hood beats low and fast over the stubble, eyes fixed forwards. A reed bunting creaks out its notes from a sapling alder, two greylag geese with carrot-orange bills raise a racket in the nearest, landward, field, which Dad informs me used to be a pool rich in birdlife until the owner had it drained. Water, which seems fixed, can appear and disappear very suddenly, in a field, in a coal seam, in a remembering eye turned on the past. There are so many birds here, and of so many species, that I exclaim in delight. Numbers of tree sparrows and yellowhammers have collapsed in my lifetime, and I haven't seen either in a long while. On the nine-hour train journey from Swansea yesterday there were periods of twenty minutes or more when, looking out over huge, bright-green and hedgeless fields, I saw no birds at all.

In so many places the silent springs we were forewarned of from the 1960s onwards are already here. They coexist in time and space with the few remaining patches of relative abundance such as here at Holywell. We live in chronological disorder, the old continuities snapped, but sometimes through the damage the past rises up in us suddenly and leaves truth-telling water on the blankness of our faces.

In its variety and abundance this strip of land on the Northumberland coast is so healthy as to resemble, perhaps, the landscapes of the 1950s, when dad was a boy. In diversity is resilience and health, and here there is so much to see and marvel at. The colours on feathers and in the heads of the grasses that blend and wave together in a perpetual movement of wind, light and shade. The flags of pools capping a mineshaft, the bright oceanic sky whose light replenishes the human spirit. What rises in Dad now is love and sorrow for his father and mother, and watching him I feel suddenly that I need to concentrate very hard on scanning the reed beds. We walk here through unruined fields of sunlit sleet and galloping month-old foals, over a slab of coast caried and cross-hatched with mineshafts in which lie beyond any hope or intention of retrieval 200-odd pickaxes, snapping tins, wristwatches forever out of time, the bones of a pony who had to go into the darkness. The North Sea wears at it all with its battery, and sea birds seeking shelter from pelagic squalls come to rest on the blind water of Holywell pond upon which bob the goldeneye, gadwall and wigeon watched from the bank by father and son.

And not for the first time I am aghast at what human beings have done to the world, but because we are here in this particular place in which my family has had a stake, the feeling of responsibility is close, personal. As far back as we have gone, and notwithstanding the other professions recorded by the censuses – the carters, farm labourers, bus drivers and butchers – every root of my family tree is implicated in mining and the glass, ceramic and metalwork industries that it fuelled. The miners of this country, local and migrant, went digging down there – under the Pennines, under the valleys of south Wales, and here, beside and under the North Sea, for the bodies of plants and animals that died over 300 million years ago. And in doing so, unknowing, they were agents of that Great Acceleration whose rate and trajectory must now be corrected though it be already ever so late.

They are, of course, blameless. We cannot pin our crisis on them. The miners, hard-pressed just to emerge uninjured back into the light and to provide for their families in the years before any kind of state welfare, could not have known how things would turn out. And if there were, even then, a few seers – Blake perhaps, Ruskin and Morris – there seemed not only no time but also no need to act on their warnings. For the land was still varied and abundant. Wasn't it still a Paradise, an enchanted ground? Certainly, the immediate landscape of the mines was despoiled, and the damage lamented by anyone with a heart, but after all, the land around was fuller of life than we today can even imagine. When the shafts were sunk there were many millions more birds in Britain. But the coal went to fuel the engines that extracted yet more coal, oil and gas, and that rate of extraction today is many hundreds of times what it then was, and while Admiral Delaval won fame fighting colonial wars the planet underwent its first poisoning. And more roads were laid, more houses built. And when the bodies of the Hartley dead had been in the ground for only fifty years, plastic was invented, and then the nuclear bomb.

Dad and I walk all morning, talking of the past as we go, with the tape machine quietly churring the whole time, our electronic, dis-embodied witness. After a while we leave the sea-light of the fields and descend to the humid green shades of a wooded dene, scooped by Seaton Burn as it makes its way to the ocean only a few miles east.

A couple of weeks later, when I listen back to the recordings made today, I will notice with surprise just how faulty is my memory, and how much I had forgotten. Just as when I'd replayed the recordings made of my visit to Mum, little over a year before, I initially heard only a dreadful crackling and panicked that there had been a technical error or that our conversation had been effaced by the wind seething into the mic. But after a few seconds, cutting through the distortion, from out of the tiny device comes the song of a chaffinch echoing in a high beechwood, a fortnight and 300 miles ago. Infilling the void behind the chaffinch I then hear again the sound of Seaton Burn before this too is displaced by a different sound – the approach of footsteps, and then a human voice:

'Nae owls?'

I had forgotten about the two birders we'd met that morning, broad-accented men, dressed for the weather, who'd directed us to a hollow tree where a tawny owl had lately been found roosting. We'd looked, there and all around, but hadn't seen it. On the recording it's obvious how Dad's accent broadens inadvertently as he replies.

'Naw. Naw. [A pause.] But we live to fight another day.'

There's an amused 'Aye!', and then friendly valedictions. So many of the birdwatchers I've known have been the most disarming combination of knowledge, enthusiasm and shyness.

When the birders had moved on, I'd asked Dad whether he was aware, as Mum had been in Eardlem, of a class or culture difference between him and his peers at grammar school.

'It's not something you really think about at the time but yes,

I think so. There was a feeling on some more or less unconscious level that the other kids' parents, particularly the fathers, were professional people. But I was good at sport, you see, and that's always a great leveller. If it wasn't for the sport, the rugby and athletics, I think I'd have felt more ill at ease.'

I ask him about books. Were there many in the house in Gloucester?

'Very few, but my mam used to *eat* Mills and Boons, breakfast, dinner and tea. I almost said lunch and dinner then.' We both laugh. 'But I used to have bought for me, and I think it was in preparation for the ten-plus and eleven-plus, revision guides and primers with arithmetic and word puzzles. And *I* devoured those, though I can't think where that interest came from.'

I tell him I remember some of his books in the house of my childhood. There were about five shelves' worth above the coffee table and the stand for the TV. In time I took them down, and still remember the force of encountering Kafka, Sartre, Solzhenitsyn. He must have gone through an existentialist phase. 'Confess', I demand, 'that you wore a black turtleneck and smoked Gauloises.'

'I think I probably did!' Dad tells me about his Spanish teacher at school, a Mr Hunt, who introduced him to Miguel de Unamuno, and who in retrospect he partly credits with making him more socially aware. 'Mr Hunt encouraged me to read beyond the syllabus. And he conducted a lot of his lessons while practising his ground strokes with a cricket bat in front of the class. "Lovatt! Hablas Espanyol?" "Si senor!" He was great, he was a good lad.'

I've never been fond of Sartre, but thinking about Dad's teenage existentialism called to mind an essay of Sartre's on the fiction of William Faulkner. I'd read it long ago, but the thrust of it had stayed with me. In this essay, entitled 'The Sound and the Fury', Sartre finds in the American's writing a model of time very different from the ordinary. For Faulkner's characters, time 'does not assume chronological order. It is, in actual fact, a matter of emotional constellations'. According to this idea, what we call the present is really only the piece of the past currently upper-most in us, and what we remember has nothing to do with the order in which we have experienced things, but depends instead on the mysterious and persistent resonances that cause certain images to recur in our lives. 'Whence,' continues Sartre, 'the absurdity of the chronology of "the assertive and contradictory assurance" of the clock . . . It would be wrong to think that when the present is past it becomes our closest memory. Its metamor-phosis can cause it to sink to the bottom of our memory, just as it can leave it floating on the surface. Only its own density and the dramatic meaning of our life can determine at what level it will remain.' This sounds to me like a stereotypical piece of French intellectual blather, but I think the gist, the truth of which I'd just been reminded of only too keenly, is that the mind is not a tape recorder.

When I looked this essay up and reread it I couldn't help relating it to what Dad had said about his jigsaw puzzle life. The more influential for being unspoken, the common conception in the secular West is that our lives run in straight lines from beginning to end. Moreover, a society obsessed with individual aspiration and self-realization encourages the illusion that we can create our bespoke selves, laying our lives down like roads, linear and predictable. Yet with his seventy years' hindsight, Dad had described his life not as a road but as a jigsaw puzzle. Born by the Tyne, he had been uprooted at ten years old to Gloucester, before a combination of ambition and chance took him to Bir-mingham and then, via marriage, to Eardlem, unguessed font of his ancestry, and then finally – but who can say? – with his second wife back to his birthplace.

The first move, to Gloucester, had happened when his father returned home from the navy in 1960 and found himself out of work. The navy then offered him another tour, but my nana, Nora, who had raised the children without their father for most of the last twenty-two years, forbade it. Through a friend's friend Norman learned of a match factory in Gloucester that could use the expertise he had gained as a ships' boilerman. I like to think that in taking on my grandfather the factory owners also hoped they would share in the good fortune of someone who had joined the navy in, of all years, 1938, and who had returned undamaged from action on a number of frigates, destroyers and minesweepers. So Norman, Nora and three of their four children moved down to Gloucester, joined a year or so later by their eldest child, Norman junior, who had stayed behind to honour his contract as a shipbuilder on the Tyne. In relating all this to me, Dad made it seem like a story, moving forwards in time from one point to another. And of course we can't but make stories of our lives in this way: narrative is baked so deeply into us that we'd find it very difficult to accept a story *as* a story if it were told in a fragmentary, arbitrary and non-chronological way, the way you make a jigsaw puzzle. But the lesson of Faulkner and of Sartre, understood intuitively also by Dad, is that a life is *not* a story, though neither I nor anyone can help making it appear so in the telling.

Dad's jigsaw remark had been made in the context of his thinking about the consequences of various major life decisions, notably the move back to Tyneside. In retrospect, he could now understand his life, in Sartre's terms, as an 'emotional constellation' in which it was the choices he had made, or that had been made for him, that comprised a pattern whose elements had been invisible to him in the moment. These choices had made up the 'picture' of his life, just as the individually more-or-less obscure pieces of a jigsaw puzzle add up to a coherent image. But with this fundamental difference, that whatever meaning our lives may eventually have for us, whatever pattern or picture they may retrospectively reveal, is never determined in advance. The jigsaw box has no illustration on its lid. In this sense, the apparent coherence of our lives is 'made up' also in the other sense – the sense we use to separate a fictional story from a 'true' one. We progress without certainty, following what is variously called accident, intuition or fate. If Dad had not met my stepmother, he probably would not have returned to the north-east, and the pattern of his life would have looked very different but, and here's the thing, no less meaningful.

And if I had married someone from Eardlem and moved 'back' there, for that reason would I have become any less lost, and the meaning of my life any clearer? Would I feel any more fulfilled? I don't think so. I recalled Alan Garner's confident formulation that belonging was 'a subtle matter of owning and being owned', which suddenly seemed to me too passive. Perhaps returning to live among the family roots does confer one kind of belonging, maybe even a rare and special kind, but how can one possibly be sure of it in advance? There are, after all, other decisions, other choices to be made, all of which can add up later, when seen in the rear-view mirror, to other kinds of meaning, other ways of having belonged. Don't we each have to make, in the end, by living and acting, our own enchanted ground?

13

The walk around Holywell had been productive in ways we couldn't have foreseen and so, not wanting to return indoors just yet, we agree to drive the short distance down to the coast at St Mary's. It's a spot I know fairly well and Dad like the back of his hand. It's a special place for birds, perhaps unmatched anywhere in Britain for its variety and for sheltering species now absent elsewhere. At home in Swansea, at any time of year, my phone will vibrate as Dad sends over his latest photograph from St Mary's, of a merlin or short-eared owl in winter, or in spring and autumn some dishevelled rarity strong-armed from its flight-path to America or the Arctic Circle by a North Sea gale. There's a large colony of grey seals here too, and almost daily sightings of dolphins. On rare occasions, with persistence and a great deal of luck, you may also see the Orkney pod of orcas from this coast, as they hunt the seals, fish, squid and shark over drowned Doggerland, the landmass that connected the British archipelago to continental Europe until the sea engulfed it 6,500 years ago. By grace, but reliably, this landscape also has the most beautiful and changeable light of any place I know.

As we get out of the car I put it to Dad that he must have missed the ocean when the family moved down south. 'Yes,' he says, all the time.' As a young boy he had always played by the sea, and often on the water itself. His uncle Kenny was a fisherman of South Shields, and he'd sometimes take Dad on fishing expeditions in the company of Kenny's sons, Kenny junior and Jimmy. Sometimes they'd stay out all night, departing in the evening when the ocean was a red mirror of the setting sun. Kenny would moor between the piers and after the fishing was over and the conversation had died down they would rest under a tarpaulin on the black back of the sea while Kenny continued to pull out fish and lobster, and the laughter, songs and oaths from the dock gradually quietened and the lights of the town went out one by one. Then the night would draw its sounds in close, and to the slap of water on the bows the boys would finally go to sleep on that black cradle.

On one of these night adventures Kenny had fancied a drink and taken the boat's dinghy back to the shore, leaving the three boys aboard. Some time later the weather had turned dirty; Dad remembers the boat lurching and causing him to break an egg he'd been planning to split into the pan. Though the fishing boat was within easy sight of land it was by now too dangerous for Kenny, after a few pints, to return in the dinghy. But Kenny was well known and liked within the fishing fleet, and quickly enough the captain of a foy-boat had rowed him out to his sons and nephew, who as he tells it now was quite unperturbed by the whole adventure. 'These things shape you,' remarks Dad, and I fall silent, thinking about what has shaped me and particularly, in the absence of such experiences as Dad had, what will shape my children.

So the sea, its movement and its lights, got into Dad, and waited for him quietly through the remainder of his boyhood in Gloucester and then all the years he spent working, and co-raising my sister and me in Birmingham. We walk along the coast, between the fields and the sea cliffs. Below us, the outgoing tide raises white weals on black rocks. There's a dry bubbling sound to our left, and two plump brown birds glide stiff-winged over the footpath to disappear into the pasture on the other side, from where they continue to call. Grey partridge. Northumberland remains a stronghold for these, formerly the commonest 'game bird' in Britain, which since Dad's boyhood have declined by over 80 per cent. According to one estimate, between the end of the eighteenth century and the middle of the twentieth, it was possible to 'bag' – that is, to kill – 100 partridge for every square kilometre, abundance back then being measured unironically in slaughter. We stop to listen to the birds. The tape recorder is still running, and a week later, back in Swansea, I will replay this little scene, with the partridge calls just audible behind the rasp of wind over the microphones. And on the recording I hear myself remark again that, thanks to the partridge, is it as though we are walking, Dad and I, through the countryside of the 1950s, so that I am suddenly both his son and his contemporary in a landscape that must even then, at what we now know to have been a late hour for the British countryside, perhaps have retained an aura of timelessness.

For a moment we must have stood there in a kind of reverie, and the recording confirms that even when we had left the partridge and continued our walk, in our conversation we remained quite happily adrift in the middle of the last century. Little wonder that the dog-walkers who greet us in passing often receive late and apologetic replies: though our senses are very much alert to the partridge, to the overflying curlew and to the white fulmars bending round the black sea-stack, we are admittedly somewhat out of time today. Now I'm asking whether Dad's siblings felt the same call back to the sea. He is sure that his older sister did, and that she carried this exile with her despite her full and happy immersion in her new life in the south-west, which included more or less losing the accent that Dad never has. But his younger sister, my Aunt Karen, was too young to miss it, and the eldest sibling, Norman junior, too old.

I ask Dad what he means, and he says that Norman had left boyhood behind before he left to join the family in Gloucester, having already begun to work. So it is true, then, that there is a sweet spot of precious bonding, a period of life between around ten and one's mid-teens, in which a landscape and its child get into one another and which can be powerful enough to last a lifetime. If the bond is interrupted early, by physical or spiritual exile, then the longing may be without conscious images, and may be felt only in dreams, in déjà-vus, in moments of apparently random abstraction or melancholy, a pang in the gut that's more than merely physical. And if the person matures long enough to experience the world 'as it really is' – that is, without illusion – then though there may well be what's called homesickness, the home left behind lacks the extra specialness that comes from the complete synthesis of child and place through deep attentiveness, daydreaming and, mediating the two, play.

Before this afternoon I'd never heard the full version of how Dad's family ended up moving from Tyneside to Gloucester, but it touched so many different parts of what I was groping towards that I ask him next about the effect of the move on his mother, my nana, who, I knew, had been deeply attached to the north-east, where she had also been helped in raising her four children by a stoic and cheerful matriarchy of siblings and extended family, a culture that still persists in this part of England as in few others.

Dad replies that the wrench of leaving such a supportive culture was hard for Nana to take. All of the organic relationships of home – what we would now refer to as 'networks' – had been left behind, and no doubt the novelty of her husband's continuous presence, now that he had returned from the sea for good, had also required readjustment. Everything would have been unfamiliar, including, of course, the house that they now rented from the match factory. In South Shields she had been busy and gregarious, occupied with the younger children in the daytime and then, if a sister would babysit, enjoying evenings in the pub as a member of a darts team. Unless the weather was cold or foul she would often take the children to the beach or the promenade where they would meet by arrangement or chance with other family and friends. Now, suddenly, the diverse ecology of her social life had been thinned. In those first few years in Gloucester they would come back up to Shields on the train for their summer holidays. And when they went back down, Dad would stay here for a week or two more with Kenny and Jimmy and his other cousins. One summer, Dad is saying, he led donkeys from the fields inland for their summer duties giving rides to holidaymakers on the beach.

As dusk approaches and we follow our footsteps back along the clifftop to the car, I ask Dad whether he was aware of this same loss of physical space and sociability following the move to Gloucester. Yes, back in Shields he had always been outside. The family home was small in any case, a postwar prefab with limited possibilities for play, and he spent whole days with his friends and cousins watching men land fish at the dock, kicking a football around or even, sometimes, going birds'-nesting, seeking eggs and then blowing out the yolks, 'out of sheer curiosity'. But perhaps in his case the full shock of this element of the move was diluted by the other, simultaneous, changes affecting him, principally the move to grammar school. Wasn't this disorienting for him, though, and didn't it even set a difference between him and his parents and siblings? After a pause: 'No, I don't think so. There was a lot of pride there.' I tell him what Mum had said: that she had felt unspokenly supported by Grandma and Grandad's aspirations for her; and I ask whether it was the same for him. As curlew fly above and around us, Dad readily agrees: 'We each had parents who wanted us to better ourselves and to break out of that [working-class] culture, if you like. And I think both sets of parents felt very proud that it had happened in that way. We didn't seek any cleverness. It was just a natural development of curiosity and interest. You start reading, things like that . . . Going down to Gloucester, you don't know anybody, you didn't play outside, there was nowhere to play in, there weren't any backyards. So it was a complete change.'

And there had been a financial sacrifice involved. The cost of uniform and schoolbooks was one thing, but the grammar school also offered trips to continental Europe and Norman and Nora were determined that Dad wouldn't miss out. At this point in the recording Dad's voice thickens very obviously as he tells me of his recent discovery, not long before she passed away, that his elder sister Valerie had contributed to his education through part of the salary she received for the embroidery piecework she took on in a factory. It was in these material ways, Dad said, rather than in any overt statements, that the family's pride in his accomplishment had been shown. Only when Dad graduated from library college, with cap and gown, the full works, did his dad's pride really show, he says. 'And it was as much pride in himself and my mum as it was in me. Without that support and sacrifice that wouldn't have happened.'

It feels, now we've started it, that this conversation could go on naturally for ever. But we're back at the car and agree to leave off for tonight and resume again tomorrow. And at home it transpires in any case that there is something else very important to attend to. My wonderful stepmother, Val, has made a pie for the ages.

The next morning I part the curtains onto a covering of snow. It hasn't snowed in Swansea in the six years we've lived there, so for a few moments I simply stand still and drink it in with my eyes – the whiteness and the silence. I'm the first one up, so I pad carefully downstairs to the kitchen. A vase of daffodils is utterly still before the window-glass, making a silent ballyhoo with its peppery yellow trumpets. Just as silently, it begins to snow, and with the snow come memories of my childhood. Of the weird white long-barrow the snow made of our rockery, of going with my friends down to the main road and bargaining to help dig out the stranded cars for fifty pence a time. It seems to me that these things happened in another life, to another person entirely.

There are footsteps on the stairs, and almost before he's entered the room, Dad's voice calls out: 'Alexa, play Skip James.' Dad exclaims at the snow and unscrews the lid of the coffee jar. As he does so, the intricate fingerwork and stark, spectral laments of the bluesman are summoned from the Mississippi Delta to a snow-bright kitchen in North Shields. Our whole family has the music bug, but Dad's a hopeless case. And though his tastes are various and he'll give anything a fair hearing, his first love is the blues. But I've never heard how he came to be bitten, so as the coffee brews I ask him, not expecting the very precise answer I receive:

'I know exactly how it happened. There was a house party around my Aunt Sally's in South Shields. I must have been about eight or nine. It sounds like a cliché, but it was Elvis, "All Shook Up". And that was it for me. Then I started to go to this youth club around ten years old and all this music was being played: The Shirelles, Elvis, Buddy Holly, you know . . .'

'So this was just about the time you moved to Gloucester?'

'That's right. And like I was telling you about reading, this was another tangible way I differed from my siblings. Because we had two front rooms in the house in Gloucester. One was the room with the telly and the budgie where people drank their tea, and in the other was me putting my records on, and that's where you'd hear Otis Redding and the blues and Hendrix later on, which took me in a new direction.'

I want to ask Dad about how this music altered the wider culture of the 1960s, but he goes there of his own accord.

'The music was changing quickly, but for me it was a discovery that also went backwards, because there's this direct line between Presley, Chuck Berry, Little Richard, and then you move into black music: rhythm and blues and the blues itself. And *that* took me into interest and participation in anti-racist stuff. It developed a social interest in me that I hadn't had. I became aware of what was going on in South Africa and in the States. Became a member of the anti-apartheid movement and went to demos. That changed me.'

I ask what his parents would have been listening to at the time, and am told they both loved Mario Lanza on the radio. Dad identifies a significant class contrast between his parents' love of Lanza and my mother's parents listening to Carla Bergonzi and Mirella Freni.

I imagine this slight, bookish ten-year-old boy, transplanted from his boyhood home to Gloucester just in time to be buoyed up by a wave of music and politics. I think of how the humane internationalism of the anti-racist movements responded to and met with a backlash of prejudice and grievance, some of which was rooted in the fear that immigration would uproot established communities, and how in some cases this really was one temporary effect.

I ask how all this blues and R 'n' B was received in the white working-class family home, and Dad surprises me by saying that it represented a continuity with his own father's attitudes. The pub- and darts-based culture that they had enjoyed in the north-east in time transferred to their new surroundings in Gloucester. With one of the older siblings babysitting, Norman and Nora would go to the pub on a Saturday night, and when it came to last orders Grandad would typically invite anyone they'd met and liked back to the family home for another drink. And these invitees would be from all backgrounds and races. 'Remember your grandad had been all round the world in the navy. He was colour-blind.' There's a pause: 'I got a lot of what I have within me from my dad's open-mindedness.'

Coffee downed, Dad ushers me to the car. I've an early train to catch, and he's giving me a lift to the station.

In the passenger seat, half listening to Skip James, who has followed us in, I think about Dad's life in overview, from the time he left Tyneside. And this time I consider it in cultural terms, for what it says about twentieth-century British society. In Gloucester he was the first member of his family ever to get into grammar school. Alan Garner has written that when he went to grammar school 'my family was, in the abstract, delighted that I was going to "get an education", just as I might have been going to get a car. For them, it was a concrete object. That deep but narrow culture from which I came could not share my excitement over the wonders of the deponent verb. To them it was an attack on their values, an attempt to make them feel inferior. A shocking alienation resulted, which we could not resolve.'

My situation and that of my sister was rather different, in that both of my parents had already left their homes to attend college in Birmingham. Rather than a sudden schism, I experienced rather a sort of slow stretching, like an elastic band pulled further and further, until the break had come naturally, as I now under-stood, with Grandma's death. And in truth, the Williamses and the Lovatts differed also from the Garners in that none of our family had worked the land for several generations, and in us the lode of urban, cosmopolitan culture, with its accommodat-ing respect for grammar school and university education, was strongly present, not *even* in Grandma but *especially* in her, with her cryptic crosswords, *Countdown* and Puccini. She was the def-inition of educated working-class, proud but entirely without ego or entitlement.

Dad was in greater danger from his break from the past, but in his case the shock of the move itself, of the change from the coast to the city and the new experience of grammar school, seems to have been lessened by the generosity and egalitarianism of his parents and siblings. If you have a father who will invite anyone home from the pub, then transgressing class boundaries must be much less of a big deal. And Dad made good use of his educa-tion. After leaving school he moved to Birmingham in time to play a considerable role in the then-rising wave of enlightened policymaking, in both central and local government, that spent unstintingly on adult literacy, inner-city libraries and expanding book-stock, which his own talent and interests enabled him to ride so that in time he became one of the principal agents of this cultured policy that in my lifetime has been quite deliberately dismantled by people of very narrow culture who fear most of all that it may reveal what they feel to be their own inferiority.

We pull up at Newcastle station. If the snow fell here, too, then it has melted so completely that it's as though it had never been. Dad gets out, we hug, and then I'm through the barriers and onto a train heading west, to Carlisle, and then back down to Wales.

14

March 2023 and I'm travelling through Somerset by train to visit my friend Anita. When I had first felt drawn to identify myself with the 'poor pilgrim' of Paul Robeson's singing, it was as a way of temporarily placing myself – in Ian Hamilton Finlay's terms – in relation to the fixed point of Canaan, which represented in a necessarily unanalysed way the notions of homecoming, purposefulness and a return from the exile of disenchanted ground.

In a literal sense, to figure myself as a pilgrim in search of Canaan had felt silly, at best. But if I had worried too much about that, and been deterred by it, then I don't know whether I would have been able to make the progress that at first I'd felt so tentative about claiming but which by now I was more and more inclined to believe in. As I had passed blindly – that is, by instinct and luck – through the stages of recreating Eardlem in memory, learning a new appreciation of and sympathy for objects, visiting Mum and my old family home, then Eardlem for real, and most recently the conversations with my dad on Tyneside, the metaphor had responded by filling in many blanks for me. If I had interrogated it at first, it would have been silent, but now if I mentally asked, for example, what I was in exile from, then it was plain that I was exiled from my childhood, or more exactly, from my childhood faith in an unfragmented, enchanted cosmos and my own oneness with it, as exemplified in my experience with the buzzard and moon on a Welsh hillside long ago. And if I asked 'What is Canaan?' then the answer rose up at once, 'Canaan is the place where you can be purposeful.'

In another way, too, and most satisfyingly, the metaphor was 'coming true' by incrementally, without my first even noticing it, replacing an *idea* of pilgrimage with the *act* of pilgrimage. When I had visited Mum, it had not been in my mind that it would be a step towards revisiting Eardlem; nor had I fully understood why I had travelled up to Dad. Certainly, I had been aware of wanting to ask him about his feelings as one whose life has sent him on a circular road back to his birthplace, and I had also felt a more or less speakable urge to follow in the tracks of my ancestors who left Eardlem for the more profitable but alien coalfields of Northumberland. But the revelation of the still unspoiled landscapes up there, all Dad had told me about his formative experiences, both natural and cultural, and perhaps especially his own metaphor of the jigsaw life, had helped me to define what I was looking for in ways that I would not earlier have been able to articulate. If the pilgrimage metaphor had once seemed unsubstantial, it was by now roomy and richly alive. Metaphors are attracted to other metaphors, and love to shine into one another, revealing yet more connections.

So it was, for example, that I could by now equate the black cracks of despair, those fissures connecting personal lostness to planetary ruin and the land of the dead, both with the cracks that connect and in a sense make whole the image on a jigsaw puzzle and also with the British railway network – those black lines on the map that enabled my forebears to find new enchanted ground and could perhaps now also do the same for me. Rather than suffering these cracks passively, I was now travelling them. I really was a pilgrim, and it was not silly. That felt hugely important to allow myself. The land of the dead was real all right: it was still everywhere in evidence in so many of the landscapes I passed through, in the forsaken towns and in the resignation on the faces of the people – *my* people, as to my own astonishment I one day caught myself thinking; but it could be traversed and understood, and there were many places and people that it had not yet claimed. Such were my thoughts as I set off from the station at Swansea, bound for the Wellington home of my friend Anita.

As the cormorant flies, the distance between our houses is very short. The Gwent Levels and the Somerset Levels were once contiguous across the floor of a tidal floodplain rich in plants and animals. The plain was hunted by Palaeolithic people whose bones have been found in Gower caves and in Gough's Cave in Somerset. Around 12,000 years ago the valley was inundated by the ocean, forming what we now call the Bristol Channel, though I prefer the old name of Severn Sea, which is still the meaning of the Welsh *Mor Hafren*. Until the late 1950s the grey-green channel was scraped white by three paddle steamers and I could have visited Anita by boarding at Mumbles and disembarking at Clevedon. In our present era the best I can hope for is that I will not have to wait too long when I change trains in the tumorous excrescence that is Bristol Parkway station.

I'm rarely down this way, and I look with interest and great pleasure at the landscape of the Levels, so very flat and green, where brightwater ditches replace hedges as field boundaries and sometimes an egret hoists itself up, legs trailing, like an origami bird rising from a green baize box. It's been raining for weeks, and as I approach Taunton the River Tone is rampaging above its banks, shambling like a Chinese New Year lion, brown and sullen and deadly swift, taking wild sideways chomps out of its overwhelmed banks. At the station Anita is waiting in her tiny V.W. After great hugs she drives us down to her home in Wellington.

Anita's father is Bengali and her mother English. She was born in Calcutta but spent most of her early life in Britain before following her career to New Delhi. I first met her in 2017, soon after she had returned to England and settled down in this small Somerset town. She knows that I want to ask her about her return to England and how she has negotiated her own sense of belonging, but we agree that such things are best discussed over wine. For now, she wants to take me to a special place. The rain is holding off, and after three hours on the train I'm also keen on a walk. So it is that we drive straight to Fox's Field.

As Anita will tell anyone who enquires, this is no ordinary field. Not that any field, anywhere, is unremarkable – we share that firm belief – but the story of this one intimately connects the past, present and future of Wellington. From the mid eighteenth century the town was an important centre for Quakers, and one of the principal Quaker families, the Foxes, still makes cloth here. In the early nineteenth century Thomas Fox and his wife had a fine house built for themselves, and established or renovated nine mills nearby, the largest of which, Tonedale Mill, employed over 3,000 people. At its peak of production, Tonedale Mill manufactured enough cloth in a fortnight to stretch from Wellington to Swansea. Dwindling output continued into the 1980s, by which time globalization had pushed most clothmaking overseas. The Fox family arranged housing for the millworkers, and it's in one such terrace that Anita lives. The Quaker commitment to humane conditions led a little eccentrically to each home being provided with an apple tree, a pear tree and an outdoor toilet.

Tonedale Mill still stands, though only just. A vast, wrecked, land-going liner, it lies becalmed in the fields at the edge of town, romantic with Victorian brickwork and rumours of owls. It is a sublime ruin, as emphatic a memento of the industrial past as it's possible to imagine. Just as many cathedrals occupy places sacred for millennia beforehand, so the mill is built on the site of an earlier, wooden, mill that was destroyed by fire in 1821. Even with the coming of electricity, water remained the mill's principal lifeblood, taken from the Tone and also its tributaries Westford Brook and Rockwell Green Stream. Basins, weirs and sluices still feed the factory's shell, the lovely old brickwork, oak and wrought iron now seeming as natural to the place as the ivy and bramble that are slowly swallowing it, even as its own great bulk causes it to sink each year, millimetre by millimetre into the earth.

Bats spool from it, pigeons woo in it and kestrels bring sticks to their nest on its slender chimney. And behind this colossal monument to the industry of an earlier age is Fox's Field, now managed by Transition Town Wellington, an environmental charity which Anita chairs and into which, along with many equally committed volunteers, she pours endless time, enthusiasm and skill. For the last eighteen months, in a process still ongoing, the field has been managed with a view to turning part of it into a forest garden. As we shuffle and leap along the puddled footpaths, Anita talks about a workshop she recently went to – intended to spread the word about forest gardens – in which the host asked the attendees to close their eyes and imagine their vision of Paradise: 'And what they *all* basically came up with was a forest garden. A place of natural and perpetual abundance where you could pick fruit off the trees and which was a mixture of wild space and cultivated space.'

For Judaeo-Christian religion, at least, the exile from the Garden is irrevocable; there can be no return to it in this life. Yet at the same time, as an imagined place of variety and abundance, of leisurely cultivation and cultivated leisure, Eden, like other religions' visions of Paradise, is an archetype and as such independent of history. In the circular time of myth, what is behind us may also be ahead of us, and the ideal of Paradise can be summoned into the present at any time, not by any mystification but by repetition of the divine example of performing loving work on the land. The ritual aspect of sowing, tending and harvesting will ring true to many a gardener.

In the middle of the field is a roped-off area of mulch and black plastic sheeting, and wire sheaths protecting many dozens of saplings. I ask Anita what is growing here, and she recites it by heart: sumac, rose and broom, sage, juniper and sea buckthorn, blackcurrant, hazel and plum, autumn olive, hawthorn, apple and Asian pear, medlar, fig and Chinese date, bladder nut, persimmon, morello cherry, cornelian cherry and pepper tree, sweet cherry, quince and mulberry. None of this is random: all the plants on the site are either edible or good for pollinators, useful as nitrogen fixers or for green manure. Anita sounds excited as she names the plants, much as I suppose God must have done, way back, and she sweeps her arm around the field to include the whole scene.

I venture that the mulch won't be necessary in the longer term.

'Yes,' she says. 'This is what permaculture is all about. We're not planting a garden; we're designing an ecosystem. There's lots of set-up initially, but all the nutrients the plants need will be provided by the ecosystem itself, and in a few years we'll reach a point where the whole thing is basically looking after itself.' She continues: 'I increasingly think that the way to look at these things is in terms of reciprocity and relationship. One of the main principles of permaculture is that everything has multiple uses, so something can be nitrogen fixing *and* a great windbreak and produce food or flower early enough to attract pollinators to the next thing that flowers. Take these hay bales, for example.'

Anita walks me over to one of the oblong bales that rest on the black plastic sheeting.

'Okay, so these are mainly here to hold down the plastic that's suppressing the rye grass monoculture, but we thought that since we've got them for a year or more, we might as well use them as big raised beds to grow veg in.'

I'm surprised that the straw provides enough nutrients, but

then Anita explains that they augment it with coffee grounds, chicken manure and compost from the municipal dump.

'Then we massage it all in!'

'Rather you than me.'

Anita grins and makes gleeful shampooing motions with her fingers.

We continue our walk, exiting the field over the brook and then forking back into a smaller but much wilder field, heading for the back of the factory. The brook is invisible, but it's given away by the line of alders that grow alongside, from the tops of which I can distantly hear the silvery tintinnabulation of finches. The grass is very long, and Anita tells me that in a recent survey, eighteen harvest mouse nests were found here in just an hour.

'Harvest mice split grass lengthwise, like you split a ribbon, and weave them like that' – here she makes intricate movements with her hands – 'whereas field voles chop their grass into lengths. Their nests look quite different.'

We have only been here for half an hour, but already I have learned so much. I'm struck by the range of Anita's knowledge, yet even more so by its intimacy. For her, seemingly, every plant, and everything that can be learned about it, is connected. The forest garden may be barely a year old, existing almost as much in imagination as reality, yet it is evidently growing out of a cultural ecosystem of knowledge and practical care. Continually, as she was telling me about the work that has gone into the field, Anita emphasized that it is a communal labour; she referred frequently to the friends and colleagues with whom she looks after the field, researches its past and plans for its future. Though I had come here to learn how she had 'found her place', there was an ever-present sense that, for her, the place and her sense of belonging to it was practically inseparable from the community of which she is a part. By the end of my visit I would have a powerful new understanding that belonging is much less like a singular noun than a plural verb: less a state than the sum of many purposeful activities, something daily renewed together in achievement of a common goal.

Glad to leave the wettest ground, we labour up a bank that leads to an artificial pool, shaded by willows and surrounded by a raised carpet of dog's mercury, a plant whose slightly sickly green leaves give fair warning of the strong poison it contains. It is a welcome sight, nevertheless, since it is an indicator species of ancient woodland. On the other side of the pool a wooden rowing boat lies half capsized in wild garlic, and beyond that is the grand house, still in use by the Fox family. We walk on to the back of the mill, where a sluice leads down from the leat cut that channels water to the mill wheel. Afternoon light, dyed greenish by its passage through the tree canopy, strobes and wavers at the lip of the sluice. The sluice-gate itself is lovely, of deeply creased wood fixed with rivets of black iron. I remark that it's as much part of the landscape as the trees and the water, and as we pause in the roar of the leat, the conversation turns back to imagining Paradise as a forest garden.

Such is the impression the place and Anita have already made on me, so clearly does she *belong* here, like some benevolent and energetic genius loci of the field, all flashing eyes and flailing arms, that shouting above the water I hear myself hazarding that we, too, are part of Paradise, though it goes against all the evidence that the world would be better off without us.

'If we go, we'll be missed, won't we? Even though we're the destroyers.'

'Yes! A forest garden is a happy and productive way of being human in the natural world, which is actually benefitting from us being there. And the Earth *would* miss us. Because consciousness of the kind we possess . . .'

'. . . adds to it.'

'Yes, because to be looked after, to be appreciated, who wouldn't want that? For beauty to be beheld. It's an actual fucking *thing*, you know?'

She laughs at that, and I, laughing with her among the dog's mercury, agree that it really is an actual fucking thing.

We walk on a little and then stop to look at the mill. On the brick sills of its many dark-eyed windows, amorous pigeons have been set spinning by spring hormones. They wobble as they revolve, the green and purple of their engorged necks splendid in the light. They look and sound ridiculous, but they neither know nor would care. They are simply getting on with life. As I watch them, I think about what I have seen and heard in the last couple of hours and again feel that something has shifted, not so much in my conscious understanding but on an altogether deeper level. It would be too strong, too eagerly seized, to claim that in this quiet minute of looking at the mill and the pigeons I feel some healing take place of the psychic wound I sustained on that long-ago commute to Bath; yet all the same I'm aware of a change – perhaps the first apprehension that peace is not to be sought in rest and ease but in the possibility and achievement of meaningful work.

I could rationalize this feeling if I chose, and explain variously to myself why it should have come upon me at just this time and in just this place. Most obviously, the mill itself and all that its kind once represented – industrial modernity, the uprooting of populations and environmental despoilation – now lies obsolete in the long grass, loud now not with whirring wheels and the shouts of workers but with the ecstasy of wrens and the bubbling love songs of the pigeons. There are consolations here, no doubt, about the resilience of nature and the inevitable passing of humanity's harmful works. But this didn't feel like the true 'lesson' of the mill, nor of the walk with Anita. After all, the mill's owners, inspired by Christian beliefs, had shown a pretty benevolent face of capitalism, balancing the drive for profit with attention to the welfare of their workforce, even down to providing their gardens with fruit trees. And in harnessing the stream to turn the mill wheel and power the machinery, hadn't they, too, been creating a new ecosystem, one which required a balance between human beings and the natural environment? No less than the pigeons, the people of the mill – owners and workers alike – had been just getting on with life. And it came to me then more clearly than ever before that this is what we also must do. That the true dereliction is to allow ourselves to be appalled into inactivity by all the destruction going on around us. Since we are part of the world too, and are supposed to be here, we had better get on with living, learning all the while from the past. We have a job to do and we must do it as well as we can.

No more than a minute must have passed since Anita and I had fallen silent to watch the mill, and all of these new feelings were unspoken, yet as if she had read my mind she then sighed and told me that, for her, working on the earth was something redemptive. Her own activity, and that of her co-workers in Fox's Field and the Transition Town movement more widely, was among other things an expression of their conviction that our species belongs in the world, and that we are not after all an unnatural blight upon it but must instead work with it, look after it, culture it. And such a conviction also gives her hope and purpose, as she explained:

'It's vital because otherwise I'd go out into the natural world thinking, "Oh no, we've really messed this up. There's no birds, there's no insects. It's just terrible. In our lifetime. On our watch. And we've known about this for ages and allowed it to happen. It's unforgiveable." But the thing that gets me out of bed in the morning is thinking, okay, we have a forest garden. There's something we have that's creating forage for the birds. It's creating an actual possibility that there'll be butterflies. It's actually restoring something that was there, before it was turned into a monoculture for cattle.'

'In other words,' I say, letting her words irrigate my own halting thought process, 'you're working within a mythic archetype where humans are at the centre, not because we're more important but just because, since we happen to be human, we can't do it any other way. But all the time with the knowledge that our humanity depends on not cutting ourselves off, not disenchanting ourselves, but in cultivating, working constantly on these caring networks we share with other creatures.'

We have left the shade of the trees now, and are carefully making our way sideways back down the soggy slope. Anita glances up at me.

'Okay, getting very philosophical and Indian about this: in the Vedas and in ancient Indian culture there's *purusha* and *prakriti*, right? And *purusha* is the witnessing awareness and is generally seen as male, and *prakriti* is the life and everything and stuff – everything that can be perceived – and that's generally seen as female. But there's something about the witnessing awareness which is itself an act of creation.'

'Yes,' I say. 'And for us the world only exists in act, doesn't it? It's in the unity of the knower and the known, the seer and the seen, that the cosmos exists. I mean not the physical universe, necessarily, but precisely the cosmos as a place where humans can live and contribute.'

'Right! Which is why whenever I'm talking about this I always come back to the idea of reciprocity. You touch something and it's touching you. We see with our eyes because our eyes are things in the visual world that other things can see!' She grips my shoulders suddenly, and we both nearly fall down the slope. But we are animated and laughing.

'Yes. We think of ourselves as subjects and forget that we are objects too. But this is common sense, isn't it? Or it ought to be. And this is what disenchantment is, right? You're being alienated from your own common sense. We've been taught to doubt it and we're not using it for its right purpose.'

By now we've walked back round to the front of the mill. The rain has returned to replenish the puddles, which this time in our excitement we don't think to avoid.

And Anita is saying, 'What you keep repeating is "sense", but our senses have been systematically undervalued and underused but once you come outside and understand that other things are sensing *you*, that they're sensing their world, and that intelligence is actually all over the place, it becomes simultaneously more heartbreaking and wounded and just awful, and infinitely more wonderful . . .' She pauses as a train howls by on the Plymouth–London line. I wonder whether anybody on board has noticed us here, two small figures standing in a wet field.

Then, when the train has passed, Anita finishes her sentence. 'Because,' she says, 'everything is *alive*.'

By the time we get back to the car we're both excited by the talk but exhausted. We agree on a siesta and to reconvene in the evening. Just before I turn in I step out into her back garden, long and green and provided for by the Quakers. On the wooden decking are sapling trees grown from seed and in the middle of the garden two ash trees, male and female, preserved as if by a miracle from dieback. Finches flit around their tops, while wood-pigeons and jackdaws overfly them. It is, I think, very much like Paradise, at least as projected through the English imagination. Then I go back inside and fall into an easy sleep. After a slow rising it's time for casserole and to uncork the wine.

15

Anita smiles. 'Right, Lovatt, what do you want to know?'

As she pours the wine I prepare to ask what drew her back to England from her successful career in India, and how she feels now about that part of her life and inheritance. I will tell her that I'm interested in where she feels she belongs – is it in India, where she was born, or the south-east England of her childhood, or is it here in Wellington? But first I tell her what I have learned so far on my odd personal pilgrimage across disenchanted ground, and my feelings for Eardlem. I talk about Grandma, and my new understanding that while lifelong bonds with places are forged in childhood, it is possible to put down new, deep roots even much later in life. I mention how the objects I inherited from Eardlem helped me to think more clearly about fellowship and belonging, and I share my grief for a time when the natural world seemed much more part of our lives than it does now.

Before replying, Anita sighs, and then she reaches to the far end of the kitchen table and from beneath a heap of bills and other papers draws out a Collins guide to birds from the 1970s. Even before I open it I feel excitement building at what I know I will find, and sure enough, when I see the illustrations, into which my childhood self poured so much rapt attention, it is like a long-buried part of me floating up from the past and fitting back into place. All I can do is smile and say, 'I remember this.' It's written on her face that Anita feels the same way.

'Yes,' she says simply, 'the illustrations are so vivid to my childhood. It belongs to my brother Sanj. He was the bird buff. But we were all members of the Young Ornithologists' Club. I remember we went all the way up to Loch Garten to see the ospreys. But more widely the connection to the landscape was through my mum. It's all to do with her enthusiasm and explaininess: "There's a stinging nettle; there's a stitchwort." We were always out on walks.'

For the next hour we talk non-stop, my questions following the flow of her thoughts. She tells me stories of her childhood in England, and then we move on to the years she spent in New Delhi, the character of the city and its hinterlands, its climate of torrid heat followed by long relieving rains, how she made friends there and also met her partner and gave birth to her son. Anita's memories of the place are full of affection, for the city, the people, for India itself. 'So what was it then, in the end, that made you come back to England?'

The light is fading in the kitchen, and the wine is dangerously on the ebb. A click and rattle from the cat-flap and in minces Alfie, her owlish and perpetually startled-looking cat. He catches sight of me and pauses mid-step, left forepaw wavering. There is a long pause before Anita answers. She says that there were very many reasons, as there always are, all mixed together and hard to separate. But finally, what she missed most of all in New Delhi was contact with the natural world.

'I really felt like there was a plant inside me that just wasn't being watered, and all of the other reasons for coming back to England were all very understandable, but quietly, on the inside, I was thinking I just want to see bluebells and trees turning in the autumn, for that natural beauty to be there when I opened my eyes, and in Delhi I found myself searching my entire field of vision for something for my eyes to rest on that wasn't concrete.'

Anita is speaking fluently now, without hesitation, and though her eyes are on me it is also plain that she is viewing something inward and intimate.

'I did try. I used to miss my parents' garden terribly, and I wanted to be able to garden where I lived. And I had this fantasy that I'd be able to have this little patch in the colony that I lived in, which was built on a grid system so that all the flats looked into a central garden. So I got permission from the residents' welfare association to do some gardening in our little garden. And the gardeners who looked after the garden . . . the idea of a *memsaab* actually digging or planting something . . . The gardeners were all like, "Okay, what the fuck is going on? a) There's this woman doing something on our patch; b) she clearly has no idea what she's doing; c) it's our job but we can't be rude to her because we're underlings and she's the elite; d) she has no tools and – just to reiterate 'b' – she's got no idea what she's doing." And there's me trying to dig this soil to plant a peepal tree which I'd been growing in a pot on my balcony.'

'And did you succeed? Is it growing there now?'

'No! It was a complete failure, because I didn't understand the seasons or the soil or the plants. I put a fork into the earth and it was like I was in the middle of a building site. There was really nothing that I could describe as soil there. It was rubble. I had to wonder how *anything* can grow in this. And I didn't even know what the plant was or what it needed, whereas if you give me any kind of English plants, a sweet chestnut, a bunch of forget-me-nots, a nettle, I kind of know what it needs.'

Given that she knew how odd it would seem to those around her, the impulse to go out there in the yard and start planting must have been overwhelming.

'Yes. I just desperately wanted to be able to grow stuff. I wanted to be able to feel like I was part of the natural world there, and the only way I could do that was by doing a bit of gardening. It's not something I explained to people because I barely understood it myself and also it sounds so soppy, but I really missed the landscape and I really missed being able to name the trees. I just wanted to be in a beechwood'.

'And when you did? What was it like when you did get back into a beechwood?'

'Absolute heaven! I was just so happy every day.'

'So when I met you in 2017 . . .'

'Yes . . . I couldn't believe that anyone in England could have the gall not to be completely grateful all the time for all this natural beauty, even though we're one of the most nature-depleted countries on earth.'

Our conversation continued a short while longer until the daylight left the room and we cleared up the dinner things and each retired. But I lay awake a long time, despite the wine and the full day before it; long into the night my mind was turning over all that Anita had said, about India, about the British landscape and her work for Transition Town Wellington. Above all about the importance of *doing*. Something about the way she had described trying to cultivate the unpromising ground in the Delhi compound had marked me with a strong visual impression. As clear as an illustration from a book I could see the plot of rubbly soil under siege from the tower blocks on all sides, and in the centre Anita, kneeling with spade and sapling. But it wasn't just about the absence or presence of trees – after all, she'd told me that there are very many trees in Delhi. Coexistent with her need to see natural beauty was her need to *act* upon the Earth. After she'd described the gardeners' incredulity at her efforts, she'd gone on to stress just how much manual labour generally is depreciated in India. It's not just gardening – the idea of choosing to work with your hands, if you could afford to pay someone else to do it for you, is seen, she said, as crazy. And then she'd told me about Indian friends of hers who, equally sceptical at first, upon visiting Anita in Somerset had been able to see and understand the joy she finds in work that back home would be viewed as demeaning.

'Will people fucking stop clearing stuff up! It's not rubbish it's where someone *lives*!'

It's the following morning and we've come back out to Fox's Field to plant a tree. I'm catching a train back to Wales in the afternoon and the original plan had been to spend the early part of the day walking in the Blackdown Hills, but after all that had transpired yesterday it would have seemed unsatisfactory, even plain wrong, to continue *talking* about acting on the land without actually *doing* anything practical. Besides which, yesterday's conversation and walk through the fields had left me genuinely itchy to work with my own hands. So I asked Anita if we could defer our planned walk in the Blackdowns and first plant one of the oak saplings potted in her back garden. She seemed pleased with the idea, and said that the best place would be by the stumpery on the edge of the field, where a previous sapling had been inadvertently lost to a mower. I know what a stumpery is because they have one in the Botanical Garden in Swansea – a great heap of tree boles and rotting wood that provides a refuge for invertebrates and fungi. But as we load the car with sapling, shovel and scythe, I'd never have believed that a stumpery could be the cause of so much excitement and so many enthusiastic expletives. As we approach it, though, Anita's smile fades and a long shadow falls across the oaths. It seems someone has been tidying up; apparently some logs have been removed altogether, while other stumps have been set upright for use as seats.

'Bloody hell! It needs to be untidy. That's the whole point!'

With a bit of rearranging most of the damage is soon rectified and I can see the stumpery in more or less its proper condition – and fully appreciate what a dank haven it must make for creatures of all kinds. By long habit my imagination always sets to work when I enter a particular landscape. I can't walk past seaside scrub without scanning for migrant warblers, or emerge from woodland onto grassland without mentally populating it with green woodpeckers. So it is that while Anita takes up the scythe I find myself rhapsodizing about the weasels I see whisking about the stumps, the jackdaws poking among them and the grass snakes skulking under them.

'You're right about the snakes,' she calls. 'I saw one here with my brother last summer. The stumpery is just about the richest habitat we have here, and it's all because it's dying. Have you heard of morticulture?'

I say I haven't, but the name speaks for itself and I already love the idea.

'It goes back to what we were saying yesterday – about making connections and seeing the potential in everything. I've been learning a lot about curated decay as a way of actively managing places like this. I suspect one reason we've been too slow to think about the wonderfulness of dead and rotting things is that we've got such a messed-up view of death generally. We shun it, our own and everything else's.'

'But in the midst of life . . .'

'Exactly! And we need to let go of these false expectations of permanence and start to embrace the morticulture in horticulture.'

I look up and see the mill. 'This applies to human ruins as well, doesn't it?'

Anita follows my line of vision.

'Yes, there's this fantastic sense of grand decay about the place, which is great for wildlife but also very beautiful and, well, apt.'

'The decay belongs here too. Death belongs here, and it's all good.'

When Anita has scythed down an area of grass I finally get my hands on the shovel and push down into the dark, loose soil. The sapling is young – younger than my own son – and the hole needn't be very big. I shake it gently from its pot and press it down into the earth, feeling coolness rise up into my fingers and forearms. How long it has been since I touched soil, smelled it, rubbed it between finger and thumb, saw it infill with colour the wrinkles on my hands! As I straighten up I catch sight of some mature oaks on the other side of the field – centenarians at least – and into my mind comes a version of the 'picture' I saw last night of Anita scraping the soil between the New Delhi apartment blocks. Only this time I see the two of us here, right at this moment, Anita and me with scythe and shovel, but foreshortened and small as if seen slantwise from a height. We are in the front of the picture, beside the newly planted oakling, but by a puzzle of reverse perspective it is as though the sight-lines of the picture converge on us from the rear. My inner eye is compelled backwards, beyond us, not to one fixed point on the horizon where the desire-lines of perspective must usually converge but rather away from us in every direction, encompassing, in the near-ground, the stumpery, but then widening out and seeming to accelerate and blur so that the whole tousled, light-filled field, the mature oaks in the middle distance and above all the vastness of the ruined mill are as it were converging on *us*. Imagine looking though a peephole but being suddenly aware that it is you who are observed by everything 'out there'. I don't think Anita noticed my momentary absence and I didn't remark on it as we gathered up our rucksacks and made our way slowly back to the car.

In the five years I've known Anita, and particularly in the messages she and I, with our friends Pippa and Michael, exchange within our WhatsApp group, she has talked often about the peace and beauty of the Blackdown Hills. Now, in the few hours before I leave Somerset, she's keen that I see them for myself. The hills are clearly visible from Fox's Field and a very short drive away. We park at the side of a lane and ascend on foot into the ecclesiastical grandeur of a mature beechwood. Underfoot are last autumn's rust-green leaves; beside us the smooth silver buttresses of the trunks rise and rise. Following them with our eyes we lose ourselves in a tangle of interlacing filaments. It's like being inside a brain. It *is* a brain. It knows that we are here, and we are welcome. I feel my own mind wake to meet it. It's always been like this: whenever I'm in a wood I become more aware of my surroundings, perhaps because I become less aware of myself, and don't get in the way of my own senses. My *purusha* and its *prakriti* seem to rub along better in woods. Simply, everything seems easier: sight, hearing, memory. Language, too. I feel language rise in me like sap, so that I only need to look at the complicated trees for a minute before my pencil starts to mark my notebook with sentences. 'Thick, muscled boughs,' I write. 'Tortuous and serpentine. Scabbed protuberances, fissured and reticulated, enjoined at junctures by grotesque, suggestive bosses!' It's great fun – some kind of release – and it runs alongside my more mundane thoughts as though it were a mind of its own.

And the wood and its surrounds are full of life. Woodpeckers and nuthatches call; woodpigeons, comely and absurd, fly past clumsily with sticks, arcing away from the wood. In a clearing we scatter a small flock of chaffinches, but what's that over there? Something tiny in the fork of a hazel, but now rising, not by hops but by small uncanny increments. It looks like a bubble crawling up a rose stem in water, or how you imagine a clot of cream might slowly blunder to the top of the jug, or like the way raindrops on a train window, if the train is travelling at great speed, under pressure of the shovelled air will sometimes shiver *up* the pane. Only one bird moves like that: a treecreeper! And it's neither a bubble nor a clot nor a cloud-coloured droplet but the bird's white belly that's hugging the trunk, the creature's otherwise brown plumage all but invisible against the bark. We stop to watch, passing the binoculars between us until we've both had our fill of it – odd little person!

We walk on, clear of the wood and onto a heathland plateau. So it was from here, last summer, that Anita sent the ecstatic text-message dispatches about the nightjars. It's good to see it with my own eyes. Anita, in red tracksuit top and walking boots, careens purposefully from the track and into the boggy heather, to show me a pool where sundews grow; I point out a stonechat pair on the gorse. On these liberating uplands the conversation freewheels here and there, taking in tales of our families, political correctness and the likelihood of adders. We stop by a mossed-over bank of earth tickled and riven by beech roots – perhaps a medieval field edge gone feral – and take turns photographing each other excitedly gesturing at stoat holes.

Back on the open hill, admiring the mix of habitats before and below us, we come back naturally to talk of ecosystems and the practical philosophy behind the forest garden. I say that the myth of Eden above all stresses abundance, but I'm coming to realize that variety is just as important. 'Yes,' she says, 'and it's not important for its own sake but because variety fosters resilience.' All over the world ecosystems are failing because variety has been stripped away for the sake of farming monocultures which, however, are inherently susceptible to natural disasters precisely because they are an imposition upon the natural landscape rather than a living part of it. Small-scale horticulture and forest gardening, though, as I saw yesterday, encourage abundance *and* resilience precisely by multiplying connections.

'And something else you've made me realize,' I say, 'is that not the least vital of these connections is the action of gardening itself – all that scything and pruning and composting and digging and planting brings humanity back into the web too.'

'Yes. And it's also so *good* for you. The companionship of working on the land together with other people is good for society, good for localism and good for your own mental health. Natural resilience and community resilience go together, and it's resilience we need to be building, right? Not . . . happiness or feeling good about ourselves, or anything like that.'

'Yes I see that. It's about restoring links, and you can only do that by *acting*.'

'Exactly. It's about what you do. And through acting you start to see differently too.'

'And that's where the re-enchantment starts, isn't it?'

'Yes!'

We have come to the furthest point on our walk – a viewpoint beside an old stone beacon, one of those once set ablaze to warn others of threats from the sea, to make them prepared and call them to action. We stop on a bench to take in the view. Using Wellington as a marker, I calculate that we're looking north-west. So the highlands on the near horizon must be Exmoor, and the grey thread beyond it – the Severn Sea. Even beyond that, though, what I first took for pillowed cloud turns out to be another line of hills. Wales! A look at an internet map confirms it: where we are sitting aligns directly along a north-west axis with Swansea. I've learned so much from Anita – twenty-four hours can scarcely have been spent so richly – but now it's time to go back over there, across the water. To go (there, I've thought it . . .) *home*.

16

There's a place I'm coming to know a little, where I stay a few times a year, as often as I can. It's a pottery, with the potter's house, a long wooden workshop, a kiln shed and outbuildings, a gallery for sales and a couple of cabins for guests in the narrow garden that runs along the bank of a small river called the Burry Pill. The pill is tidal a mile or more up from the sea, so twice daily the water flows back the wrong way, and sometimes cormorants flap stiffly above it, looking out of place in a wooded valley, their carved faces like pew-ends, expressionless and set. The woods are wet and very old. They're privately owned and you can't walk in them, but you can cross the pill by the road-bridge at Cheriton, or a half-mile upstream by what's called the packhorse bridge, which was built in the reign of the first Elizabeth. If you stand here in winter twilight it is very easy to imagine that the cold mist that rises from the water to envelop the bridge is mingled with the breath of the long-departed horses, but if you think you hear hooves, it will only be a stone working loose and clopping along the river's cobbled bed. Once, while waiting here for woodcock to leave their damp squats in the wood and embark on their weird looping flights, an injured fox limped past me unknowingly, less than six feet away.

Having first caught a bus halfway down the Gower peninsula, there are two ways to approach the pottery, both very beautiful. The inland path descends from the bog-topped sandstone spine of Cefn Bryn, from whose crest you can see the beaches of the south coast that in summer draw holidaymakers from all over Britain. But always my head is turned the other way, north to the vast marsh-flats of Llanrhidian and Landimore, with the Burry Inlet gleaming beyond and, on the far bank of the estuary, the Carmarthenshire hills and Llanelli looking improbably regal in the downdraughts of clear light. In winter those hill plateaus are often topped with shining snow, and at any time of year when the sunset lights them from the west the combined effect of light and distance lends them a hushed and spiritual glow beyond the power even of the wind turbines to dispel.

Yes, this is a great place to observe how light behaves! The sunlight gushes through cloud holes in great slathers, whimsically drapes or divests the mountains of golden altar cloths and slinks tigerish across the marshes and the long dark brindle of conifers going out to Whiteford Point. Here the tide is ripped back and forth over sandbars and skerries and to look at it you would be right to conjecture a bitter litany of shipwrecks. On the wall of the Pilot pub in Mumbles there is a map marking all the remembered disasters, naming all the ships of conquest, commerce, industry and pleasure that are homes now for posses of blank-eyed bass and the inlet's famous oysters. But the straits are nothing to the sun, and from the tops of the Bryn I smile to see it pounce in one bound from Whiteford to Pembrey, flashing across the water and even stealing a little of its dazzle to wash the windows of the terrace houses on the far shore, before ascending to recline again, louche on the distant heights.

But even the sun can't do much with the ancient valley woods. They wear a gloomy look even at a summer's noon, when, though flush to the warm light, a stubborn vapour still clings round the trees. The ridge, the valley and the shining water of the estuary appear utterly distinct zones, yet they're threaded by the waters of the pill, which rises here on the wet moorland then gains pace on its descent through the valley until at last it drains to the ocean in stroppy brown meanders.

Beautiful as it is, though, I don't normally come down that way. Almost always I catch the bus to Llanrhidian, and after crossing the churchyard and the ancient stone stile squelch my way around the hem of the wooded hills that overlook the marsh. Long ago these were sea cliffs, but in the long wrestle between land and ocean the shape of the coast has changed countless times, as of course it changes still, though the span of mortal thought can barely make sense of it. Yet in another way this landscape is very obviously changeable, for tides wash it twice daily, covering everything bar the phlegmatic marsh ponies that stand planted and apparently indifferent even as the cold currents swell around their hooves and hocks. You can witness it five, ten, twenty times and never quite become used to the sight of a herd of horses apparently walking on the water of the Celtic Sea.

We never know which walks, when first taken, will in the end become familiar and dear. I first came to the pottery the winter after Grandma's death, on what turned out to be the coldest day of the year, or for several years. The old woods were stiff and white. The puddles I crunched round and the troughs left out in the fields were rhino-skinned and rimed with ice. An unnerving knocking from an unknown source, echoing across the frozen marsh, turned out to be a goat's horns clattering against a bright green bucket of feed as the animal dunked its head. The swedes it might normally have eaten were presumably too hard even for a goat's teeth, though it was clear from the orangish scrape-marks on their pates, and the dark corridors of bent grass leading down from the wood, that badgers were still coming to them. That first day, the walk which should perhaps take two hours lasted twice that, in part because the going was so difficult, but also because I had to stop every few paces to absorb with all my senses the beauty of the winter marsh. Far, far out, above the gleaming silver strip of the inlet, shorebirds arose suddenly and oscillated, light to dark, in a scintillating double helix, giving form to emptiness. But chiefly I remember the hawk I came upon in a bare tree right at the edge of the marsh. They are normally so shy, and I can only assume that hunger had made her incautious. Though I write these words years later, and despite everything I must have thought and experienced since, I can return to her without effort, as though through an open door. I see more clearly than I see these lettered keys the light trembling in the diagram of thorns where she perches, herself the colour of twigs in winter, glowing like a drawn scimitar in the dull January light.

I barely made it to the pottery before dark, and I was done in. I set a fire in the log-burner, opened the laptop and put on Górecki's *Symphony of Sorrowful Songs*. When I stepped outside to fetch the chamber pot from the woodshed a thrush was singing down the darkness and despite the cold I kept the door open for a minute, because the alchemy of the bird and the voice of the soloist struck a shiver right through me that I wanted to sustain. It felt like a draught of something nourishing that I had been too long without. Afterwards I climbed the wooden ladder to the mezzanine bed, expecting deep and immediate sleep. Yet on the other side of the skylight, six inches above my sleeping face, a mouse was busy between dusk and dawn. Even when I must have passed into unconsciousness, the scrabbling of its feet across the corrugated metal fed plot lines of drama and flight into my shallow dreams. At eight I pushed the window to learn what all the excitement was about. Seemingly moss, which had been neatly removed from the base of the window and taken some-where else for purposes unknown.

At first I thought I came here for the bird life and the beauty, and the peace its surroundings afford my mind, but although all that's important I've come to realize that the pottery does me good chiefly as a model of order. Micki, the potter and my host, is the presiding spirit of this orderly universe. Micki's stone house, her workshop, her studio and the row of closed and open sheds and shelters that house the kilns, wood-stacks and tools together constitute a cosmos. I don't mean that it's a sealed space. Last time I stayed here a lorry delivered a load of timber from Monmouthshire, bound with ropes and sticky with frost from crossing Bannau Brycheiniog. But the wood, and every outside substance and influence that's absorbed, as it were, through the cell wall of the pottery, is carefully chosen because it is necessary to its continuance, maintenance and, where necessary, gradual improvement. Everything that happens here is purposeful and intelligible, and though gaiety is welcome, the least triviality would embarrass itself. Neither are there any gestures nor per-formances here to attract or impress. Almost all the objects you will find, whether in the buildings or outdoors, are natural or handmade, but this fact – which might elsewhere be looked on in a self-congratulatory way as an end in itself – is less important than that, whatever they're made from, they are all *for* some-thing, and nothing is made, nor any action undertaken, without intention. My friends Mandelstam and Heine would delight in how every object is brought within the compass of meaningful human activity, and elevated by its practical, unostentatious use.

The commercial value of the cups, bowls and vases may be significant to the continuance of the pottery, but not a single pot is made solely in pursuit of profit.

Indeed, the whole way of life here, regardless of type and scale – the record-keeping and draughtsmanship, the chopping of wood and the thoughtful preparation of good food – together comprise an organic culture that actually ennobles the commercial element, respecting its importance while in no way allowing it to dominate or overreach itself into a distorting motive. Everything begins from the action of work; the priority of attention accorded to the pots ripples out into the whole ordered life of the pottery. Extroversion is alien to a place whose mode of existence arises instead from the needs of work, the 'point' of which is the drawing forth of beauty in function, the making of vessels to be used for the nourishment of people and the satisfaction of the eye and the mind in colour, mass and form.

I don't think I would have been able to communicate any of this very clearly on my first visit to the pottery in that January of 2020, less than a year after Grandma's death. Back then, in those months when the dream-beasts still haunted me nightly, and even following the unexpected clue gifted me by that aphorism of Ian Hamilton Finlay, I was still flailing for any handhold and seeking the answers to my problems in the past. It really felt, that winter, as if the breathless despair of 2017, those intimations of culture and planet in fatal freefall, had the power to disenchant my very sense of self and belonging. I was trying to fix myself in my own life, in order that I could make sense of other things, but it seemed more likely that I would never find such anchorage, never understand myself.

At intervals over the last quarter century I have returned to something Uncle Jack said to me on his deathbed, and to how he looked when he said it. He lay on his back under cold blue plas-ticky sheets, and tubes twined from him like something already had hold of him that was going to drag him off somewhere. And when he opened his eyes he said, 'It's a funny game,' meaning life, but in his eyes was unmixed bewilderment. Apart from that, I don't remember another thing about the visit, but Jack's con-fusion will stay with me always, and the only question is in what way: as an unavoidable foreshadowing of my own fate or as something I managed to escape.

This is no mere intellectual problem for me because, looking back that winter, I could see that all my life had been disorder. My love of animals and birds, of music and harmonious words and pointless beauty of all kinds, those gifts of my heredity and upbringing, had sustained me into my fifth decade. But my innate shyness and what you might call lack of investment prevented me ever really getting a grip on the world, of being part of society. It always was enough for me to enjoy how light, falling through a window, would lie breathing on carpets, walls and floorboards; or outdoors how rippled sunshine scattering back from streams and rivers would throb on the underside of bridges.

Childhood is a pool from which you can sometimes return to drink, or at least to stare at your foreshortened reflection, in rare idle moments and in dreams. But you have barely been in the world ten years before you are channelled down courses, canalized and sped up, until you reach the middle of life and feel yourself without the strength to stop yourself being pulled along. If you really struggle, and do not deceive yourself, then the best that can happen is that you will spin like a leaf in moments of slackness, and turn for a while in memory. But you will still be pulled along in the end.

And the truth is that you didn't even know that you were

leaving the cherry tree, the gnats' country dances that so delighted you, the dyed ice palaces, Grandma and Grandad and the house in Eardlem with its wide windows onto the fields. And the adult wonders how you can have been so careless not at least to have said goodbye. And you return in your forties instead, and the cherry tree is a driveway, the children are all indoors, and you feel in your blood the approach of the empty days when it will not even snow any more.

Such was the tenor of my thoughts on the first morning of my awakening at the pottery, while the coffee brewed, the logs whispered as they rekindled and outside the cabin window a robin sang from the white pear tree, dolorous and aching-sweet. But even as these thoughts came, on a preconscious level I must have sensed that the peace, beauty and order of the pottery was a countervailing influence to all this despair, because I decided then and there that I would come here again, and that on these visits I would keep a journal of whatever I saw and felt.

This was not, though – at least not at first – such an easy thing as I might make it sound. For a long time I was reticent to approach the life of the pottery in words. Compared to what I already sensed of its orderly and purposeful life, my own appeared hopelessly chaotic and ungrounded. In part this was simply because it was so much arranged around the demands of others, whether the children or after-hours editing jobs or the online timetables of my workplaces, where the holy hours are represented grimly and tellingly as a grid. But it was mainly a consequence of the lostness in my own life that I have tried to describe. All of this gave rise to a sense of unworthiness. How could someone so disoriented begin to write about the life of the pottery without feeling like an imposter – either someone posing as a resident or as some kind of envious ethnographer?

Nevertheless I was powerfully attracted to the life of this place and its people, and in the end the rightness of this feeling, plus, crucially, Micki's gradual acceptance of my presence, helped soften my reservations into a reason for tact rather than a barrier to engagement altogether.

Even so, to write about this place with the minimum of authority not to feel a fraud would take time. What do I know about designing a kiln? What do I know about working wood and clay? I can tell you a bit about Russian literature, a bit more about how to tell the British falcons apart or, on a good day, how to balance a sentence. But where is my place? Where is my *ground*? I felt keenly the bad faith of borrowed authority that I dislike so much when I smell it in other people's writing. And manifestly, this wasn't only a lack I needed to address in writing, but in living, in *doing*. For my life to have the same congruity as the life of the pottery, I needed a place within which to achieve a kindred equilibrium with everything around me – people, other creatures and objects alike. I felt this and thought again of Alan Garner saying that everyone must know their place, and of the death-bed bewilderment of Uncle Jack, who, cuckooed on Grandma and Grandad, had perhaps always felt his own lack of place. And finally I thought of a saying of the Sri Lankan philosopher Ananda Coomaraswamy, who held that the difference between the Platonic (European) forms and the Indian ones was that whereas the former are like abstract and ideal diagrams, forever just out of reach, the latter are forms of sentient activity in the here-and-now. This made instinctive sense to me the first time I read it, miserable in the disorder of my earlier life, and it still holds good now. The patterns of conduct that we are meant to follow are not to be sought without, but should be daily enacted, whatever they may be.

The pottery wasn't my place, and I wasn't going to pretend otherwise. But as a model of order it felt like it could be a means of my regaining enchanted ground, not as an idealized place to be sought 'out there', but in the form of a relationship between what I was doing and the place I was doing it in, no matter where on the Earth that might be. Besides, in and beyond the garden of the pottery was something I *did* know already, intimately and effortlessly: for there lived the birds and other animals, going about their business alongside the human life of the place. These two sorts of ecology – the human one that has at its centre Micki's creative action at the potter's wheel, and the natural one of the garden and woods, the pill and the wild marsh – not only overlap but sustain each other, the natural world providing peace and inspiration necessary to the art, and the pottery providing nest sites and feeding places for its non-human people. And I, over time, and as I came to cement this conception of the place, felt my position shift from that of an interloper to something more connected, even to a tentative sense of semi-belonging. And with the confidence I took from this new relationship I began to see that the proper way to approach it was through my own attentiveness and my own art of writing. And so, on short and long walks away from the writing table I began haltingly to compose a journal of this most beautiful of wild, worked places, which had begun simply as a 'retreat' from where to write articles and this book, but steadily became instead – with a conscious nod to Hamilton Finlay – somewhere to plot an advance back into connectedness and health.

17

I leave the cabin early, and there's nobody about. The light is cold, flat and drear. It's mid February 2022. The news is of an impending storm, named Eunice, but here in the deep lane between wooded banks there's no sign of it yet. If the woods can sense it, they seem unperturbed. They are brown and sagging like old sofas, shapeless under vast drapes of wild clematis and fringed low down by the ragged golden antimacassars of hazel catkins. I make a mental note to remember where they grow now, while it's so obvious, so that come September I can go straight for the nuts. But I won't do it – never do. I'm not sorry, because the autumn hazel-hunt is fun and the satisfaction greater when, back in the cabin in the afternoon, I pour out hazelnuts from my raincoat pocket into one of Micki's grooved and shapely, ochre-coloured bowls.

I could never be bored here. No matter how often I come there is always something that quickens thought and feeling. On the path this morning are molehills where none were before, dew-damp upthrust tumps of reddish soil, new under the sun. And in the same sunlight a lamb lies sleeping not far from its mother. The farmer will have been up all night, perhaps for several nights in a row. There will be losses, but if all goes well enough then 150 lambs will be born here. Yes, I know what will happen to them. I continue down the path, past the black mouth of a pipe from which silver water slackly lolls, mimicked on either side by a foolish crowd of harts' tongue ferns. Out in the open now, I suddenly feel the wind. I look up at the ash and oak tops, where last year's leaves are fluttering back along their twigs as if to escape their exposure and take cover in the thicker canopy.

The storm gathering just offshore halloos up the estuary and the marsh flats, causing the reed beds to wince and brindle, and the blanched light to wobble on the weirdly shaped pools. The hen harrier is here, even as I had hoped. I have a déjà-vu. Could she have come in last night's dream? I've never seen one this close. The gale's ferocity tilts her inland to hunt right against the margin of cultivated ground. She flies into the wind, with constant hesitations and readjustments of her long owly wings. Now she is right above the swede field. With my back to the hollow-sounding wood I steady the binoculars to watch how she tucks down her head to get a better fix on whatever quakes there. Her face is impassive. She hunts back and forth between the fields and the reeds for half an hour, but even in this relatively sheltered bay of the marsh the wind must make prolonged flight tiring, so she touches down to rest. But now she is too close to the rooks of the wood, who cannot abide her. One after another they dive and force her airborne again with repeated attacks, and then they rise to joust in the wind, twenty feet up, as a single ray of sunshine puts a taper to the marsh and the whole landscape ignites. I could continue but force myself to turn back. There's writing to be done, but I surprise myself by the awareness that I'm also missing human company.

At the pottery I pause to watch the giant cherry tree creak and sway above the cabin where I'm staying. If it falls this way, all that will be left in the morning will be man-smeared matchsticks.

I lower my gaze to the understorey. The wind is lesser down here, but still strong enough to buffet the blue and great tits that foray from the bushes to the wire feeder. That they can fly at all is incredible, weighing as little as they do. Using their tails as rudders they launch into the air, and when they make it to the mesh they grip it tight with grey-black claws.

In the studio Micki is absorbed and illuminated like a saint at her wheel by a prescient shaft of sunshine. When I tell her so she says, 'Well I did try praying, but I wasn't sure who to pray to.' She comes back with me to look at the cherry tree. The forecast is for the storm to peak in the early hours. We try to calculate which way the tree would fall, and she asks if I wouldn't rather move to the other cabin, but I say I'll stick it out. I don't know why, but I'm certain it won't come down on me. I'm concerned about flooding, though, since Eunice will coincide with the highest tide of the year. But Micki knows from experience that we'll be fine. She points out how little rain there's been of late, and how shallow the pill. There's only a real threat to the pottery if the water coming up is met by an equal flow coming down, and then over the banks it comes. 'But not this time, I think. Not tonight.'

Micki returns to work, sheltered behind Radio 3 from the increasing volume and menace of the gale. I'm readying to do likewise when the sound of an engine curves around the drive and Sal the woodswoman emerges sideways from her old car. She's here to batten down the tarps and make sure the wood-stacks are stable before the storm breaks. Sal is a regular presence here, valued for her calmness and knowledge. Her judicious axe is often heard echoing from the other side of the valley. She knows the different capacities of the site's five log-burners, and cuts the wood to appropriate lengths for each. You can learn a lot in five minutes' conversation with Sal. Neither of us is a great talker, and perhaps we're still a little shy of each other's company, but from our splinters of conversation I'm starting to appreciate the pottery's economy of wood. I know, for instance, that these stacked logs are mostly of alder and ash. Alder is by nature a wet wood, and gives off a comparatively weak heat. It will do for the burners in the house and cabins, but it's no good to fire the kilns. As with everything here, Sal's knowledge is employed practically and with a purpose. She dries, seasons, sections and stacks the right wood for the right time, keeping it all in order. I'll never enjoy the sound of axe and saw. I'm only interested in woods for their timbre. But I recognize in Sal's measured management something I value also in writing, and it's with that thought in mind that I wave goodbye and return to the laptop.

Micki established the pottery here on the banks of the Burry Pill in 1987, using the knowledge she had acquired at college and in a period spent in India, and as a peripatetic potter in Europe, to build her own kiln. As I now know, there are kilns and there are kilns, and this one is of quite a rare and particular kind: a cross-draught, wood-fired 'beast' for the creation of salt glaze pots. In her preference for salt glaze Micki is in a sense staying true to her roots, for this technique is thought to have first arisen in medieval times in Germany, from where her father came. The glaze upon pots made with this method is a chemical outcome of the alchemy of silica and alumina already present in the clay, and sodium that is separated from chlorine by the more than thousand-degree heat of the kiln. The interaction of these elements is highly dynamic and unpredictable, and in the volatility of the firing process abides an element of chaos that perfectly balances the grounding routines of

the pottery's regular life. Over repeated visits I came to think that this balance of earth and fire is also a true expression of Micki's personality. She has written of this method of firing that 'It's not a process you can ever totally control, but experience teaches you to bring together all these elements to create the best possible chance of a good outcome.' Although her modesty would forbid her from saying so, Micki is recognized by her peers as a master of her methods and one of the finest salt-glaze potters at work today.

All night the black woods howl and roar. I lie awake listening to the hollow sound. Nevertheless, only half my attention is on the storm, with the other half turned inwards. I can feel the weight in my body of all the years of anxiety I have carried with me. Yet something about the pottery, and the life lived here, not only by Micki but by the other potter, a young man called Chris who I'm just getting to know, by Sal and even the occasional gardeners who stop by to prune and graft for a few hours, take coffee and leave – yes, the life they live here, its purposefulness, order and dedication that I keep coming back to, is loosening and lightening the great dark mass I drag around. It feels as though the more time I spend in this place and among these people the easier the load becomes. I'm still a stranger here, and I chide myself in the dark that it's too early to tell whether it will have a lasting effect on me. But even as I think this, it seems dishonest. There *is* something powerful here that my penchant for renunciation shouldn't be allowed to ignore. Yes, I am still an outsider, but somehow I am starting to sense with certainty that this place is the nearest surrogate I have found for whatever it is I have lost.

In the morning everything was calm, so when the cherry tree came down we didn't expect it at all. I was standing looking at the pill when behind me came a splintering boom, so loud that my balls cowered and my stomach dropped into to my boots. The tree must have been fatally weakened by the storm. It fell, as we'd hoped, away from the cabin, but in such a way that it completely blocked the footpath that runs along the bank behind Micki's land. I hurried round to look at it. It had split off about six feet up from the roots, and the jagged yellow heartwood shone out, frank and austere, looking like solidified torchlight. Micki had heard it too, and we stood for a while, looking at it in silence. I asked her who would move the tree and she said the farmer would. I remembered how exhausted he'd looked when I'd seen him in the lane the previous day after the night's lambing, and how, the first time I'd met him, I'd gauchely asked him what he did on the farm. There had been a pause and a thin smile. 'Survive,' he'd said.

Sal has come back to restore order to the garden, which is snickered with fallen twigs and larger boughs. I feel myself in the way, so I set off for the marsh to look at the flood-tide receding. The hedges are filled with birds. It seems wonderful that any should have survived last night's ravaging, and I don't see how they can have slept, but the hedgerows are loud with their cries. Sparrows are the carefree traders, blithely buying and selling in the glittering temple of the morning, but robins repine in the margins, murmuring sad religious verses.

When I reach the marsh, a weak sun breaks through and lies down on the salt pans. In these strangely shaped shallow pools the light is both lacquer and plumb, burnishing the surface but also sending rays down into the dull olive water, illuminating there the submerged hoof-prints of the marsh ponies. These prints in turn provide hideouts for small brown fish that flit in fear of my shadow. On the bank of a creek I watch dew ascend as mist. A pale vague movement on the pasture pixelates through the binoculars into a flock of thirty or more goldfinches feeding silently on the ground, tugging at seeds and stalks. They move to a new patch with erect clockwork hops. A few hours ago all this was ocean.

From the edge of Cym Ivy marsh I watch a kestrel beat over from North Tor and then turn suddenly to hover over an oblong of tall grass. It's marvellous how her frenzied wing-beats work to keep her head and body so still. So much energy is spent to pinpoint the flame of life inside the vole that fidgets somewhere below, beneath an arch of bent stalks. If she can transfer it to herself, and do the same thing over and again, then she may survive to bring into the world new famished kestrels. Truly the marsh is a buffet for predators of all kinds, and every time I come I stop before the wrenched feathers of some small bird that's been taken by merlin, peregrine or hawk. The bodies themselves are rarely found, as the raptors take them away after plucking. Just once I saw the skeleton of a wading bird – a redshank, I think – that for some reason had been overlooked. I was utterly stopped by its beauty. I would like my writing to be like that: as small, as bare, as intricate and unadorned.

Night brings no relief to small birds, for the woods that mantle the tor are a haunt of owls.

After yesterday's confinement by the storm I feel like walking miles and miles. I quicken my pace – how the gristle in my hips enjoys it! – and make for the pine forest that straggles down towards the tip of Whiteford Point. On the lane I stand aside for a logging vehicle, on hire to thin out the twentieth-century plantations that are now marching on the adjoining dunes. This whole area was formerly an artillery range, and dramatic signs warn against handling any metal objects protruding through the sand. The threat is real: the bomb squad have their own table at the local pub. The sentinel pines, officious but kindly, warn you in their own way by dropping grenade-shaped cones all over the wood and right down to the edge of the dunes.

It's heavy going here, but I prefer the dunes to the easier route along the beach because you never know, when cresting them, what you might flush from the hollows. Some bowls hold fresh water that attracts jangling wisps of goldfinch and bullfinch, as well as nourishing the roots of alder saplings and chutney-coloured thorn-bushes. Where the spit narrows the high tide mark is visible as an intermittent line of plastic and black wrack. After the gloom of the pines the space and light are exhilarating. I hadn't realized I'd been hunching my shoulders, but now they relax of their own accord, and I stretch my arms wide in imitation of the cormorants that stand drying their wings on the iron corsetry of Whiteford Point Lighthouse, beyond which a bank of vapour hangs eerily mid-channel of the soapy blue estuary. Out there is a blue mussel graveyard as deep as your boot can dig, and on the channel itself rafts of eider dive for shellfish while brent geese, stubby-billed and charcoal-coloured, paddle out with the tide.

I enter the bird hide at Whiteford but get no further than the doorway. To judge by the sight and smell of it, every single bird on Gower must have sheltered there during the gale. The whole place is full of the dung of what I think must be the starlings that in milder weather billet in the pines. There's nowhere to sit so I go back out again into the waning white light. When I come to the last sand of the inlet shore, where it is pale with powdered sea-shells, I suddenly feel exhausted from the walk and perhaps the suppressed anxiety of a night beneath the doomed cherry. The light is so clean here, the waving shadows of the sharp grasses so crisp and clear, and the colours of the shells so pure, that I lie down and immediately fall asleep. Perfect refreshment to be out here where no other human being knows I am.

When I wake the light has changed and I can smell rain. I will avoid the dunes and take the faster forest path, where grey roots lie beneath a shifting skin of orange-grey pine needles. I think I'm alone, but all of a sudden there's a white horse on the path, so white that she seems to glow slightly in the gloom. She doesn't look like one of the feral ponies that live on the marsh, and since I know my mythology I conclude she must have come from Annwn, the underworld. I tell her that I'm pleased to meet her, that she's a gorgeous-looking boggart and to let me pass in the name of God, at which she rolls her blue eyes under their long white lashes and releases into the needles a torrent of yellow piss. When we edge past each other in an awkward pas de deux, I see by the bulge of her belly that she is pregnant so I invoke the deity again, this time to keep vigil over her foal.

Before returning to the cabin I stop in at the pub, where I learn that the days of the gentleman rep are gone, that the cockle-beds of Loughor are being pillaged for the Asian restaurant trade, and that a certain Evans is a right cunt.

18

For a long while I was kept from revisiting the pottery by work and by illness in the family. But in April 2023, just a few weeks after my visit to Anita, I received an email from Micki inviting me to come over during the following week's firing. I'd asked if I could attend several weeks before, but with little real expectation that I'd be admitted. A firing is a very big deal. There are only four each year, and they are planned long in advance. This firing, like all of them, had first appeared in the pottery diary as a distant lodestar, but as winter came and went, and time started slipping towards it, so too did the pace of the potters' work increase and their attention converge on this weekend, when the artistic and the economic, the material and the intangible elements of the pottery meet in the blending of earth and fire, water and air in the white-hot kiln.

I know that the mental energy required by a firing permits no distractions, so I'm immensely grateful to Micki and Chris, and pledge unobtrusiveness and tact. As soon as the Swansea bus drops me off at Llanrhidian, Chris's car pulls over and he leans across to open the passenger door, smiling under his yellow beanie. I ask how he is.

'Tired. The last few days have been quite intense.'

Is he pleased with what he's got in the kiln?

'I haven't made many this time,' There's a pause and something that could be a grin. 'I've got some questionable teapots.'

'Why questionable?'

'They've got very big spouts so they look a bit goofy.'

When Micki is around Chris takes a respectful back seat, so I've rarely heard him talk in detail about his own work. But as I listen to him today I will come to understand just how thoroughly he knows the kiln and how deeply the life of the pottery has entered into him. As we drive between hedges along the quiet lanes he tells me about a particular spot in the east corner of the kiln that never gets as hot as anywhere else. Something about how in that place heat and air travel with more difficulty through the bagwall that separates the firebox from the raw pots. I feel suddenly attracted to, perhaps even envious of, Chris's knowledge – not the content of it but the very fact of it and the depth of its utility.

When we get to the kiln Micki is there to greet us, in leather jerkin and a red hat from which protrudes, like smoke, a characteristic quiff of white hair. Her manner is friendly as always, but it's clear that she is intent to the kiln. There are 300 forms in there, packed on shelves behind fire-bricks and fire-resistant silica calcium board. This is a cross-draught kiln, allowing ash to come through the shelves, so there's much more interaction between ash and the pots than in a down-draught kiln, do I see? It's an individual: Micki has learned from different kilns she's built and seen, and by now hers has a personality of its own. There are all sorts of apertures for controlling the flow of air. To avoid a big build-up of ash, Chris has made clay slabs ('with a lot of grog in them, so they're very tough') on the base of the firebox under the kiln. Airflow and ash extraction is made possible here by ashpit mouse-holes. The vocabulary of firing is rich and wonderful. I ask why the kiln is raised and learn that it's mainly for convenience and ergonomics, to spare their backs when they're stoking the fire and adjusting the inflow of air. There's a third potter here today, a young woman called Ellie who's been before and, as Micki herself did fifty years ago, spends her time travelling between potteries in a practical apprenticeship that's also a labour of love. When Chris and I arrive Ellie is checking the pyrometer, which in a homespun set-up is propped with slanting nails and bound by brown twine to a vertically suspended plank that dangles beside the west wall of the kiln. Ellie exudes calm, and seems exactly the sort of person you need in a situation as poised and fraught as this.

Although it's only nine in the morning, the firing has already been underway for fifteen hours. The kiln is preheated with gas, which Micki lit at six yesterday evening. In the middle of the night Ellie came out to check that all was well, and then it was Micki's shift again at five-thirty a.m., when the gas was replaced by woodfire. I'm nervous, feeling out of place and all too aware that my usual response to nerves is to make light of things. Not here, not now. This is not the time for fooling around. Perhaps sensing my awkwardness, Ellie invites me closer to read the pyrometer, which registers 600 degrees. By tonight that temperature will need to have more than doubled, but it's easy does it. Ellie opens the east door and feeds in one of the logs that's lying ready on a long table before the kiln.

'You need to increase the temperature slowly,' she explains. 'Then you increase it by about thirty degrees an hour at first, then gradually take it up to fifty per hour.'

Chris appears with coffee, but after a quick cup I make my excuses and head to the workshop where I set up my computer and begin to record what's happening. I need a bit of time out before I feel ready to return to the kiln.

The long workshop is quiet and full of light. It's the sort of unpreferential, frank and gracious light that gives equal attention to every object it touches. Away from the kiln I feel myself relax and I realize that I too am an object lit by this indiscriminate blessing from our remote, homely sun. I let the quietness sink into me and then look around at the other objects as though at a party of friends. I'm sitting at the long central workbench where the light lies flat and placid. Beyond it is the log-burner with its long silver flue in which the light is folded and fluted, making long distortions of whatever shapes and colours it can gather. On either side of it are four freestanding open-shelved dollies with planks laid across them, some bearing newly formed pots, the others apparently bare, and a folding screen door with twelve hooks for as many sober-hued aprons, and the bare space inscribed with remarks in pencil: 'you might have to wait some time'; '*le fond de l'air est frais*'. On the adjacent wall, also in pencil, is a diagram of the kiln, with appropriate labels and dimensions marked. I think of Coomaraswamy's dictum that 'the art in the mind of the artist, in the plan and in the finished work are the same'. As I turn my head to take in the other side of the workshop a movement in the garden catches my eye. A yellow butterfly, a brimstone just risen from hibernation, is doing long elasticated loops above the planters of rough, sea-salvaged wood in which grow rosemary and lavender. At the same time, in a still-living ash tree by the pill, a mistle thrush starts up singing his lofty, inhuman song. The only other sound is the ticking of the flue as the logs catch in the burner. Through the skylight last year's oak leaves twist on their twigs and the clouds pass over. The burner pops, the seconds tick by, a robin's song filters through the walls of the workshop and of the heart. The snowdrops are already thawing in the churchyard. The buzzard palming the air will have eggs by now in its nest in the inaccessible trees somewhere down by the sewage works.

To my left is Micki's wheel, but right now I'm more absorbed by the fantastic array of objects on the other long table. Here are pots of all kinds, bowls, mugs and candle holders, vases attenuated and squat. Other vessels hold scores of wooden-handled brushes, quiffed, compact or tufted. Shaving brushes, buffing brushes, brushes for slopping on slip. Others accommodate chisels, bevels, augers and their close kin the corkscrews, wooden spoons, pins, craft knives, candles, wooden and metal rules, cockle shells, oyster shells, wooden carding combs, masking tape, an autonomous subset or devolved region of toothbrushes, strange, duck-billed things with wooden handles and sponge heads, a hacksaw blade, clay half-moons, wooden clothes pegs and, in a wicker basket, half a dozen thicknesses of twine.

I'm so completely absorbed in this quirky parliament of objects that I don't notice Micki until she's entered the workshop.

'Do you want a job?'

'Of course!'

She leads me over to the planks, which, bare of pots, I'd assumed to be empty. Not so. Very carefully she reaches one down and I see that along its centre runs a thick stripe of coarse-grained salt the colour of fish glue. You can't have a salt-glaze without salt. But this doesn't look like any old salt.

'No. It's from Guérande. Gathered by hand. I don't know for sure, but I think it has a little bit of magnesium in it that gives a softness to the glazes.'

It's forecast to drizzle at midday, but in the meantime the salt could use some air. I follow Micki to the kiln shed and we set out trestles, then when she's gone I ferry out the salt-heaped planks, one by one, and lay them across the trestles while wrens fidget in the camelia, the pill babbles to itself and Chris, at the kiln, pulls out and replaces fire bricks, checks the pyrometer and bundles in another log every few minutes. When I've finished with the salt I go over to him and now he's standing back from the kiln so he can see the top where an orange flame flickers out of a small blowhole. He's looking for smoke. There shouldn't be any at this stage, because he wants the carbon to come out of the clay.

'If carbon is hanging round the pots then the other gases can't escape and you get bloats.'

'Bloats. Right.'

Micki rejoins us and for the next two hours I watch them work. It's wonderful to see, and for a layman like me it's also astonishing how much there is to do. To the left – which by now I have learned to call the 'west' – of the kiln is an old wooden shelving unit upon which two logbooks are set. One records the temperature of the kiln and the other is used for more general comments such as weather conditions. Both logs are inscribed every few minutes. Micki, who has changed her hat to something scarlet and gnomish, stands erect at the logbooks very much as a submarine captain might stand at her charts, intent on steering the kiln through the perils of the coming hours. For this is one of the most dangerous periods of the firing. The temperature now stands at over 1,000 degrees, and Ellie explained earlier that this is a stage at which it tends to plateau unless it is vigorously stoked with just enough wood at just the right times. If the kiln is allowed to lose momentum now, if its internal weathers slacken, it will be a difficult task to recover it. Meanwhile Chris, as it were in the engine room, is a study in concentrated action, forever stoking east or west, or half pulling out firebricks to gauge the temperature of the kiln, partly by the colour of the flames but chiefly by the condition of the pyrometric cones, thin ceramic pyramids that are ranked to melt at different temperatures. When a cone of a particular type begins to wilt, this is the best indication that a certain temperature has been reached. The

length of flame coming from the blowhole is another good meas-
ure: is it reducing or oxidizing? Is the kiln sated or hungry for
more wood? Since it's impossible to monitor cones and blowhole at the same time, I'm given this second job, which involves
standing just outside the kiln shed and barely taking my eyes
off the flame. If it dips, I alert Chris that it's time to add another
piece of wood.

Micki is visibly nervous. Chris seems calmer but by now
I know he goes quiet under pressure. Since I'm watching the
flame intently I don't notice him light a roll-up, which he holds
with astonishing deftness considering he's wearing enormous
fireproof gloves. There isn't much talk, and none that doesn't
concern piloting the kiln. The talk is quiet, matter-of-fact,
directed, elemental. It is all of ash, fire, salt, the metal oxides that
will be drawn out and dribble fantastic colours to the surface of
the clay. Micki, Chris and Ellie take turns at stoking. It begins to
rain and Micki frowns. It means a change in air pressure, a more
lively or less predictable wind. So much can go awry; there are
so many little apertures through which a rogue wind can enter to
make mischief of this stage – called 'specific reduction'; everything can make a difference and require some minute adjustment.
Chris checks the cones every fifteen minutes, trying to ensure a
balance between the west and east sides of the kiln. Every inter-
vention or significant change is logged.

The rain grows more intense and I, beyond the cover of the
shed, put up my hood. When knots of thick, dark-grey smoke
begin to pour from the chimney and wisp through cracks in
the kiln, little insects appear from nowhere to flee the fumes:
an unsteady moth and an issue of tiny, almost transparent milk-
white flies. Ten minutes later a bat is obliged into the drizzle.
Flying in low loops it crimps the edge of the surrounding trees

before landing on the roof of the gallery and disappearing through some crack.

Nothing new happens. Micki stands at the logbooks, flipping pages, studying charts. Chris never takes his eyes off the kiln. He bobs up and down at the table on which the logs rest. Through a slit in the bricks the fire is an orange bar. There is a sudden sharp sound and some quick answering movement from Chris. A spy hole brick has cracked in the heat, but he replaces it quickly. He calls across to Micki to tell her what has happened, and Micki pauses for a second before saying simply, 'That's good, Chris. Very good.' The rain shower has stopped but the shed eaves still drip, water flowing musically down the corrugated metal and watering the bank behind with its ivy and ferns. A new log sizzles. The quiet mood seems to have affected the birds; just an occasional wren sounds from the depth of the wood.

A car crunches down the drive and the spell is broken. My partner and children have arrived to pick me up. I say goodbye to the potters and when I glance back finally from the car door all three of them are standing taut in the dusk, staring fixedly at the creative fire of the kiln.

Two days later I return. The firing made a big impression on me, and I've been thinking about nothing else in the free time I've had since. One of my thoughts was that when I came back I should be wearing the last jumper knitted for me by Grandma, and I'm glad I remembered to put it on this morning.

I walk to the pottery the coastal way, along the edge of the marsh from Llanrhidian. As if in a significant echo of my first ever pilgrimage this way, among the birds I surprise on the walk is a hen sparrowhawk. She sees me, shrugs a brown shoulder and then moves off, swift as a cursor across the brown ground of the woods. It's easy to miss, but this is a human landscape too. Lime kilns gape around the base of these old cliffs, which are riddled with springs and tunnels the water has bored. Ten metres downstream from where the largest spring issues out of the ground there is the ruin of a mill, now a sombre place thick with ivy and the horrible balled fists of new ferns that have just punched, zombie-like, through the soil. But the freshwater makes it a good place to stop and wait for thirsty birds. I keep still for fifteen minutes and am rewarded. Two pairs of bullfinch arrive. Or rather, I don't see them fly in but suddenly they are just here. On creaking chains they move rose-coloured lamps within the bushes' thick glooms, and it is a while before the first of them breaks cover and flies down to the water. Such a beautiful bird. His back is the blue of the woodsmoke rising from a farm chimney, and his chest the red of all those sunsets you couldn't help but photograph. A blue tit enters a conifer. I watch it bend to wipe its beak on a twig and then flit around the soft twig clothed in needles. A raven flies over the wood, making its strange call, like the smooth insides of a cough.

From the wood the path emerges again onto the estuarine edge. An even, clement light lies on the marsh, but there is rain in the air, and when clouds overshadow from the landward side the ranks of trees put on a damp mien as if in anticipation. Through the binoculars I watch a reed bunting surfing the bowing green sea of reeds, square-snipped tail a rudder. Beyond her a black dredger waits in the inlet for the tide to turn, squat and immobile on the fields of grey-green blue. A shelduck flies off with characteristic lowered neck, as though it had been surprised doing something shameful, while in the far distance a flock of lapwings rise up and write their buoyant calligraphy on the horizon-line. How I love it here. The whole grand, tawny spectacle.

By now I am close to the pottery, trying to increase my pace through the pasty mud in my eagerness to see the results of the firing. There was a lot of rain again last night and the stepping stones over the pill are overrun by an inch of tugging water coloured grey by the clouds. At the corner of Betty Church woods and Cwm Ivy marsh I come clear of the hedges and by my very presence put three egrets to flight. We are an animal it is difficult to abide. Back under tree cover, tiny white flies drift between the wet-black filaments of a sycamore sapling still not quite in leaf, like floaters before the veins of the wood's eye staring out onto the marsh. The last thing I see before I turn inland is a grey heron at the waterside, an angular dandy in a motheaten thrift-store stole.

At the pottery I go straight to the kiln, before which seventy or so pieces have been lined up on tables in approximate order of form and size. Micki and Chris are both there and greet me in a friendly way. Circumspectly I admire aloud a brown cup, speckled like a trout and I could almost fancy still warm. It is truly beautiful, but Micki says she has difficulty with brown because that was the colour of her uniform at convent school. Chris looks happier, and gently lays out what he's made on a trestle table opposite the kilns. Suddenly a shadow flits in from outside, and then seemingly disappears into the roof. A swallow! I say that it's lucky to have Persephone's bird here as a blessing on their wares. They show me the nest it's begun to build on a high beam. They're concerned about the heat but I reassure them that the bird won't mind. I ask what kinds of wood went into the firing. Chestnut, cherry and ash. Then Chris holds up a cup of such extraordinary beauty that I know at once it must be something special. He tells me someone gave him a piece of 5,000-year-old ash wood that had been dug out of a bog. He'd used it in the glaze, and this was the result. That you wouldn't hang on to something like that, but would *use* it! This is a lesson for me.

I stay for two nights and fall more easily this time into the rhythms of the pottery, even though I'm mostly still an observer. Cutting wood. Doing the accounts. Making soup. Showing visitors around the gallery: these actions are the year-round metabolism of the place. The days are filled with writing and walking, relieved by encounters with Micki or Chris and shopping trips to the volunteer-run community shop. But in the evenings I realize that I'm lonely, and on a deeper level than thought wonder what I'm doing here. Video calls to my partner and children in Swansea are awkward and leave a wake of restless silence that bad habit wants to fill with mindless internet browsing. Rain percusses on the tin roof, breezes rattle the sapling branches against the cabin walls, thrushes in the darkening wood will soon be replaced by owls. Fire mumbles round the logs in the burner, slurring soft grey ash. The very age of this place, from which I usually draw peace, can sometimes in the middle of the night seem intimidating. The farm over the road has stood since the fourteenth century, the church since the twelfth. Lives then were usually shorter than now. Assuming an average span of sixty years, fourteen generations have passed between the builders of the church and me. The first person to have been found here on the peninsula of Gower lived 25,000 years ago – that's well over 500 generations. I was born in the 1970s, Mum and Dad at the start of the 1950s, their parents at the start of the 1920s. I think of Grandma and Grandad and of Eardlem, not so very far away in distance but irretrievable in time, and the loneliness comes again.

The next afternoon I'm walking to the packhorse bridge when I meet the farmer cutting back the ferns that are encroaching on the hay meadow he rents. He breaks off strimming and we talk about the wildlife of the valley. The otters are still about and have scared the trout in the pill so that there are many fewer to be seen than formerly. There are mink, too: his neighbour lost all of his hens to them. Back at the cabin I have smaller fauna to deal with. Two early moths rest shipwrecked on the windowsill. I coax them into an empty ice-cream tub and before I go to sleep I leave it outside the cabin door.

Overnight the weather has cleared and the wind shifted to the west. It is sunny and warm. I take out the battered enamel chamber pot and after emptying it into the far nettles glance up and notice the moon swimming hungover in brightest blue above the trees. Like the chamber pot how proudly it shines. How battered its own enamel! The visual rhyme is almost perfect. There was an overnight dew and webs shine in the pear tree. Subtle, dull green winds slouch through the nettles and other plants of the understorey. The two moths I expelled last night are for some reason still passive in their ice-cream tub. I tilt it gently into the woodpile and they stagger out like survivors of some great catastrophe.

After coffee I head to the shop to buy supplies, but decide to take the scenic route through the fields. Maybe it's the sun, perhaps it was the sight of the new pots still laid out glistening on the tables, but for some reason I feel unaccountably happy. An iron gate sings on its hinge as I pass down deep-green lanes crossed by shadow. The shadow of some raptor passes over me too swiftly to be seen. Two minutes later I come to a bush where the sparrows are still talking about it. The stile to the next field is broken, the wood rotted through, but the sun shines on it anyway. It occurs to me that this is what grace is, and I suddenly begin to laugh.

When I return to the pottery half an hour later with a rucksack full of rice, broccoli and eggs, Micki is working her wheel in the lit studio. I am just about to back out when she rises to wash her hands. Then, noticing me, and as if continuing a conversation that had just been broken off, she says, 'It ties you to one place, being a potter. The tons of bricks and wood. But I don't want to get stuck.' I ask if she is planning to move, surprising myself with the force of my hope that she isn't. She tells me, then, that she feels incredibly connected to the place, but that lately she has been aware of some kind of loosening: 'And the loosening is being hastened, I think, by how the place itself is changing. The first flood was five years ago; now they are annual.' Until recently, she had seen the river only as benign, 'but now it is somehow alarming.' Trying to keep my voice level, I ask her where she would go if she left here. There is a pause in which the light in the long room seems to grow stiller, and then she says, 'I take my hands with me everywhere I go, and some clay. The clay helps me belong to myself.' And as I hear her words, I feel that at last my pilgrimage is at its end.

Micki heads to her home, and I make my way in the opposite direction, to the cabin where I am staying. Just as I pass the kiln shed one of the swallows dips past me and up to the roof beam, and for some reason beyond explanation, for the first time since primary school, I cross myself, a smile all over my face.

Coda

Every society in history has its myths of enchanted ground, and mythic time is not historical time but the possibility of an eternal present that can be re-entered whenever and wherever we live well. Our problem – and we have made it everyone else's problem, too – is that we have accepted the wrong myth of what it is to live well. I'm not advocating going back to some supposed Golden Age; this book ought to make clear that I'm not trying to go back anywhere at all. The past has gone, and we can't belong there. I know, because I tried it.

Apocalypse, deregulated capitalism, whatever you want to call it, works by severing all prior relationships and rerouting the debris through itself alone. By debris I mainly mean us. People. And the aggravating evil is that for these new, inhuman networks to work at maximum efficiency, it is necessary to make people forget that there is any other way of living. But there is. I do not agree with Alan Garner that belonging is a subtle matter of owning and being owned. It is, instead, a subtle matter of working and being worked.

When I walked through the green desert around Eardlem I had almost despaired, but when I reached the service station and heard all the birdsong, I had laughed. For perhaps twenty, thirty – who knows? – a hundred miles around, the motel grounds were the only place which hadn't been sprayed with chemicals, and which had a variety of trees. It's no secret what needs to happen.

When I walked with my dad through Holywell and along the cliffs at St Mary's, we had walked together through the 1950s and for the duration of that walk had been contemporaries in mythic time. We were able to belong together in that time because the place itself was timeless – not, of course, in any supernatural way but in the ordinary sense that human and other natural life was allowed to go about its abundant, complex and various business there. Behind all our diminished, sad and emptying land- and townscapes are their real, thriving selves. These are the places in which we would like to belong, and we must work to make it happen, beginning with ourselves.

The story of this book began with my losing a special person and a special place, but it honours both Grandma and Eardlem to recognize that every person is equally special, and every place, too, without hierarchy or priority. This is, in fact, the heart of what all my grandparents, and my parents, my sister and I believe. You could call it socialism. It doesn't much matter what you call it, though the principle is very – you might say vitally – important.

I made a mistake in thinking that I could find somewhere to belong the way you find a parking space. It took much too long, but by 2023 I had stopped believing that belonging is something you can find, and then 'have', at all. Through Dad's research and example I had learned that no deracination need be final, and that human communities can grow and reroot themselves anywhere. And Anita and Micki, principally, showed me that belonging is in fact something you do, provided that the action is one of care or creation. It is an action, not a thing; or it only persists as a thing for as long as the caring, creative action is maintained. I'm thinking of Anita with her field and Micki with her wheel, but no less of Grandma peeling those spuds and washing up after dinner before the rest of us had even finished our pudding. Grandma didn't belong in Eardlem because she 'came from' there, but because she cared for it – not abstractly or passively, but in the practical sense of keeping it clean, picking up litter, becoming a local councillor and school governor, singing in the choir and acting in the theatre, keeping the pencils sharpened in the bureau and putting the suet out for the robin whatever the weather.

Sometimes Mum, and all of us, would look at her and ask, 'Where does she get her energy from?' But I don't think that's mysterious, either, when you remember how her father raised all five of them as a widower, keeping them alive and seeing them through school till fourteen, even while he worked night shifts down the pit. And I remember, too, in this connection, Dad saying that he couldn't think where his interest and ability in book learning came from. And Mum remarking that she was 'turning into' Grandma, and the look on my wife's face when

she remarked on our children's resemblance to us and to their grandparents. We all, all of us, have so much more available in us, so many more resources of strength, than we know.

And where do I belong now? Well, here, in Swansea. Where else? This is where I work, take the children to the beach, volunteer as a school governor, pick up litter and skin the potatoes for chips with the slightly overfamiliar, bordering-on-eerie, backwards hand-action of an armadillo-like vegetable peeler. I belong here, and may the same happen to you over there. I really do think that when we all start belonging again, that the lane to the land of the dead might be diverted somewhere much more interesting.

Note

Throughout the book some dates, and names of people and places, have been altered.

The phrase on p. 109, 'The grand homecoming that will never take place', is a quotation from *Speak, Memory* by Vladimir Nabokov.

Acknowledgements

My first thanks, always, are to Judit and our children. It wouldn't have been possible to write the book without the time you made for me. Thank you! Great thanks and praise are owed to Anita and Micki, and I hope these come through in the writing. I have learned a great deal from both of you, and I only hope I can carry myself through the rest of life with half of your wisdom and grace. To Sam Fulton, and all at Penguin, thank you for your patience while I tried to work out the shape of the book, and for your shrewd and generous editing. Great thanks, also, to Richard Atkinson, who showed faith in me at a crucial moment. When the book was no more than a mess of half-articulated frustrations Michael Malay asked very good questions and was tolerant of some very strange answers. One of your earliest questions, Michael, was 'What's the point of all this remembering?', and I hope this finished book offers at least a partly satisfactory answer. I am grateful, as always, for your friendship and support. My thanks to Kirsti and Daniel for use of the CREW room, without which everything would have been much more difficult. Finally, and most importantly of all, thanks to my mum and dad. Goodness knows what you'll make of this book, but it's for you, anyway. All my love to both of you, and sorry about the swear words.